OUTWARD BOUN
MAP & COMPASS HANDBOOK

OUTWARD BOUND
MAP & COMPASS HANDBOOK

Third Edition

GLENN RANDALL

FALCONGUIDES

Guilford, Connecticut
Helena, Montana
An imprint of Globe Pequot Press

FALCONGUIDES®

FalconGuides is an imprint of Globe Pequot Press.
Falcon, FalconGuides, and Outfit Your Mind are registered trademarks of Morris Book Publishing, LLC.

Illustrations: Jack Tom
Art on pages iii, vii, ix, 1, 19, 33, 44, 53, 59, 66, and 93 licensed by Shutterstock.com

Text design: Eileen Hine
Project editor: Julie Marsh
Layout: Sue Murray

Library of Congress Cataloging-in-Publication Data

Randall, Glenn 1957-
    The Outward Bound map & compass handbook / Glenn Randall.
    -Rev. and expanded ed.
    p. cm.
    Includes index.
    ISBN 978-1-55821-747-8
1. Orienteering—Handbooks, manuals, etc.
I. Outward Bound, Inc. II. Title.
GV200.4.R364 1998
796.58—dc21

98-18603

ISBN 978-0-7627-7857-7

Printed in the United States of America
10 9 8 7 6 5 4 3 2 1

The third edition of Outward Bound Map & Compass Handbook is dedicated to my father, a civil engineer who first taught me how to use a map and compass; to my mother, whose "itchy feet" and love of travel inspired my own desire to explore the forgotten corners of the map; and to my wife Cora, an atmospheric scientist whose constant drive to understand every subject in depth inspires me to do the same.

CONTENTS

ABOUT OUTWARD BOUND

Outward Bound, America's preeminent experiential education organization, has been a pioneer in the field of wilderness experiential learning since it was established in the United States in 1961 and has continued to deliver unparalleled outdoor educational programs ever since. Today Outward Bound provides adventure and learning for teens, adults, veterans, at-risk youth, and professionals, helping them achieve their full potential and inspiring them to serve others.

A Brief History

Outward Bound is based on the educational ideas of Kurt Hahn, an influential German-born educator. Hahn established the School at Schloss Salem in an attempt to combat what he perceived as the deterioration of values in post–World War I Germany. Salem's progressive curriculum focused on character development through physical fitness, skill attainment, self-discipline, and compassionate service. In 1933, thirteen years after establishing Salem, Hahn fled Nazi-ruled Germany to Britain. Soon after his arrival he set about establishing the Gordonstoun School in Scotland to continue his work under the motto "Plus est en vous" ("There is more in you than you know").

In 1941, in a joint effort with British shipping magnate Sir Lawrence Holt, Hahn founded the first Outward Bound Sea School in Aberdovey, Wales. The name of the school was adopted from the nautical term used when ships leave the safety of the harbor for the open seas: They were said to be "outward bound" for unknown challenges and adventures. The school not only taught sailing skills but also integrated Hahn's core belief that character development was just as important as academic achievement. Hahn's goal was to teach self-reliance, fitness, craftsmanship, and compassion as a way to provide the youth of Great Britain with the benefits of life experience and prepare them to serve their nation in the struggle against Nazi Germany. The program revolved around a series of increasingly rugged challenges designed to develop the self-confidence, fortitude, and leadership skills required to survive harsh physical and mental challenges.

Josh Miner, an American who taught under Hahn at Gordonstoun, was inspired to bring Outward Bound to the United States. Working with a small group of committed supporters, Miner founded the Colorado Outward Bound School in 1961, bringing the principles of hands-on learning and compassionate service through outdoor adventure to America.

Outward Bound Today

Today Outward Bound has expanded to thirty-six countries throughout the world. In the United States the organization has close to one million alumni who stay connected and engaged through Outward Bound's alumni association (www.outwardbound alumni.org). Central to its mission are the values of inclusion and diversity, evidenced by its scholarship program designed to attract and benefit populations that are typically underserved. Approximately 25 percent of participants receive financial support, and they span ethnic, socioeconomic, and geographic diversity.

In the United States, to advance goals of transforming lives and developing compassionate, purposeful people, Outward Bound now offers its unique blend of adventure-based programs fitted to the needs of:

- Teens and young adults
- At-risk youth
- Adults
- Veterans
- Professionals

Although programs vary broadly in target population, location, and objective, they all contain the elements that Kurt Hahn espoused as central to the development of effective and compassionate citizens: adventure and challenge; learning through experience; integrity and excellence; inclusion and diversity; social and environmental responsibility; leadership and character development; and compassion and service. For participants in any of the varied programs, in any part of the world, these core values provide the foundation for their Outward Bound experience.

THE INSTRUCTORS

Outward Bound instructors are highly trained, qualified educators and outdoor skills specialists. Participant safety is the highest priority—foundational to every program. Every course is accompanied by instructors who hold wilderness first-responder-level certifications at the minimum and who have received hundreds of hours of educational, safety, student- and activity-management training. Staff members are proficient in—and passionate about—the specific wilderness skills of the activity they teach, whether rock climbing, sailing, mountaineering, sea kayaking, canoeing, or whitewater rafting. To help participants along their personal growth paths, instructors are trained in managing groups and individuals. A vital component of every course is the instructors' ability to not only shepherd participants through individual course challenges but also to help them work as effective leaders and contributing members of the team.

Outward Bound's Lasting Impact

The impact of each expedition extends well beyond the course itself. This impact is different for each individual but can be seen in a variety of ways, including improved school performance, closer relationships with family and friends, and a new commitment to service. When Outward Bound participants return home, they bring with them a new sense of responsibility, an enhanced appreciation of the environment, and a strong service ethic that they share with friends and family. Most important, they bring a newfound belief that "there is more in you than you know" and an inspiration to act on that knowledge. In one participant's words, "What I was lacking I have found; now I have the tools to keep growing and to work hard to accomplish my dreams, and to do anything I can to help others accomplish their dreams as well."

INTRODUCTION

The novice backcountry traveler could be forgiven for thinking that a third edition of this book is unnecessary. Advancing technology, it seems, has made the craft of wilderness navigation obsolete. In 1998, when I finished the second edition of this book, satellite navigation devices using the Global Positioning System (GPS) were just starting to become readily available at prices outdoorsmen were willing to pay. The GPS receivers of the day were rather heavy, were slow to get a position fix, had no decent built-in maps, and were only accurate to about 100 meters or so because the military was deliberately degrading the signals available to consumers to reduce the usefulness of GPS units to potential terrorists. All that has changed, as I'll describe fully in Chapter 7, and some naïve wilderness travelers now think that all they need to find their way in the woods is a GPS unit.

A modern GPS receiver, with its pinpoint precision and built-in maps, is indeed an invaluable aid in wilderness navigation if the user takes the time to master it, but it is not a substitute for old-fashioned map-and-compass skills, nor can it replace common sense. Here's an example: In 2006 a pair of mountaineers reached the summit of Oregon's Mt. Hood, then got lost in a whiteout as they descended the peak. They had a GPS receiver and a compass, but they had forgotten to mark Timberline Lodge, their starting point, as a waypoint in their GPS unit and had neither a map nor an altimeter. They did, however, have a cell phone. Wilderness travelers should never count on having cell-phone service, which is often unavailable in the backcountry. Fortunately one climber's cell phone did have coverage. With darkness approaching, the climbers called 911.

The search-and-rescue leader who fielded the call was able to determine that the GPS receiver was set to the wrong map datum, so it was giving an inaccurate position fix. In addition, the GPS unit was reading out their position in latitude and longitude instead of UTM coordinates, which are much easier to use. To compound their woes, the climber's set-and-forget compass was set to 20 degrees *west* declination when it should have been set to 20 degrees *east*. That meant that when they tried to walk the compass bearing provided by the rescue leader, they were heading 40 degrees to the right of the direction they should have gone. A search-and-rescue team eventually found them several hours after dark and escorted them to safety, cold and exhausted but unharmed.

Any electronic device can malfunction or run out of battery power of course, but there are other ways that a GPS unit can fail you (or, should I say, that you can fail it). I once spent two hours trying to find a wedding reception in Indianapolis because the driver, who had lived in the area for many years, had entered "123

Washington St." in her GPS receiver when she should have entered "123 *N.* Washington St." Stories are now legion of drivers following directions on their GPS units and taking roads to nowhere, eventually running out of gas or getting stuck in deep sand or snow. Rangers in Death Valley, who seem to be constantly searching for lost motorists in the huge, desolate valley's notoriously hot, 120-degree summer months, have even started referring to these tragic incidents as "Death by GPS."

Don't get me wrong: GPS receivers are a tremendous aid when the navigating gets difficult, but they don't stand alone as route-finding tools. Here's a case in point: For the last five years, I've been working on a series of photographs shot at sunrise from the summits of Colorado's fifty-four 14,000-foot peaks, the Fourteeners. Camping on the summit is too dangerous at any time of year due to the risk of high-altitude illness. If I drove straight from my home in Boulder at 5,000 feet to the trailhead, then hiked to the summit of a Fourteener and camped, I'd probably wake up with an excruciating altitude headache or worse, if I could sleep at all. During the summer months the ubiquitous afternoon lightning storms also create a serious risk of electrocution. Another obstacle to camping on the summit is logistical: It's a lot of work to carry camera gear *and* camping gear *and* a gallon of water to the summit, only to find that there's no flat ground on which to camp. My solution has been to camp at timberline and climb the peaks in the dark. For that kind of difficult navigation, I *always* carry a US Geological Survey (USGS) 7.5 minute topographic map (the most detailed available), a mirror-sight compass, and a high-quality wristwatch altimeter. Weight is critical in mountaineering, and important even when hiking and backpacking, so for years I would leave my aging, first-generation GPS receiver at home unless it was wintertime or my route led off-trail through the woods. Today's GPS receivers are so easy to use and so versatile, however, that a modern receiver has now become standard equipment for me.

Not even the most advanced technology, however, is a substitute for paying close attention to your surroundings as you hike. Even veteran backpackers can make mistakes, as I discovered to my chagrin on a recent backpacking trip in Utah's Canyonlands National Park with my fourteen-year-old daughter, Audrey. We had decided to explore Ernies Country and the Fins, a remote area on the west side of the park. There is a cairned route through Ernies Country, but it can hardly be called a trail. Canyonlands National Park is high desert, so finding water sources is critical. Our USGS topographic map had two springs marked along our route. Before the trip I consulted with a ranger who'd been patrolling the region for more than twenty years. He confirmed that the springs were reliable in all but the worst droughts and that both springs were flowing when he visited recently. Since it was springtime and the winter rains had been adequate, we anticipated no problems.

We hiked in on our first day and located the first spring, which lay a short distance up a spur trail off the main route. At the spring we refilled our water bottles, and then we continued on and camped near the second spring. After a day of exploring the Fins, we camped again and then headed out the way we had come in. By now we knew the terrain; surely we couldn't get lost retracing our steps.

An hour after breaking camp, we emerged from a side canyon just where two sandy washes came together. Our route continued up one of the two washes. The wash heading north looked unfamiliar—too narrow to be the route we'd taken on our way in. We chose the wash that led west instead.

Half a mile later I knew we had somehow missed a turn. The footsteps in the sand, so plentiful in the beginning, had faded completely, and the terrain looked wholly unfamiliar. I pulled out the map, oriented it with the compass, and studied it. I knew where we had been just twenty minutes earlier, and I knew which direction we had been heading. To confirm my estimate of our position, I pulled out my GPS unit and took a position fix. It confirmed my understanding of our location. Obviously we should have taken the northern branch of the wash, not the western one. We retraced our steps and started up the northern branch.

But the terrain still didn't look familiar. We were heading in the right direction, of that I was sure, but still weren't on the trail we'd taken two days earlier.

Suddenly we encountered the first spring again. How could that be? To reach this spring two days earlier, we had taken a spur trail off the main route, but at no point today had we been on that spur trail. After another minute of confusion, I realized what had happened. We had made not one mistake but two. The west branch of the wash *had* been the correct branch, but we should only have followed it for a few hundred yards before leaving that wash and heading north, cross-country, following sparse cairns to the point where the spur trail led to the spring. We had missed that turnoff not once but twice. I had simply not paid enough attention to the terrain on the way out and not memorized that one crucial junction. Fortunately there were two routes to the spring: the spur trail we'd taken on our first day and a second trail that led directly to the spring from the junction of the two washes, bypassing the spur trail altogether.

Now that we were back on more familiar territory, finding the rest of the route back to my truck was easy. I kept the map and compass handy nonetheless.

It's true that I could have created a GPS waypoint at the critical trail junctions, which would have alerted me much sooner to my mistake. Even if I had done so, however, I should still have been studying the terrain and memorizing landmarks much more carefully.

Everyone who plays or works outdoors needs route-finding skills. Day hikers and backpackers will find a map and compass useful for identifying landmarks, making the correct turn at trail junctions, and estimating travel time—even if they always follow established trails. Popular trails in most national parks are usually heavily trodden ribbons of civilization, well marked and obvious, with all too many other visitors to set you straight if you get confused. Venture into the remote parts of the national parks, however, or into forest service wilderness areas, and even trails marked on the map can be much harder to follow. Trails may be marked wrong on the map or have been rerouted since the map was printed. Unsigned trail junctions are easy to miss. Lightly used trails across meadows can become overgrown and vanish completely. During a nine-day, 95-mile backpacking trip along the Continental Divide Trail in southwest Colorado, we found multiple places where the trail as marked on the map didn't correspond to the trail—or lack of trail—we found on the ground. Near Weminuche Pass we only found the right route by carefully identifying the correct side valley on the map. No visible trail led across the meadow from the main trail to the base of the side valley. Only after entering the side valley did we relocate a visible track. That same day we encountered a hiker trying to follow the same route who had walked more than a mile out of his way, with a heavy pack, before discovering his mistake and retracing his steps.

Everyone who heads off-trail, even occasionally, will find route-finding tools essential. When you are bushwhacking through dense forest, with the surrounding peaks hidden by trees, a map and compass will keep you on track. Snowshoers and cross-country skiers leave tracks, of course; but in meadows and above timberline, it takes only a few hours of snow and wind to obliterate those tracks completely. Mountaineers traveling on glaciers and large snowfields are completely dependent on their route-finding abilities (and foresight in marking their trails) whenever fog and storms move in. Sea-kayakers and canoeists crossing open water must also be accomplished navigators. Even river-runners, who always know in what direction they're heading, need to know how to use a map and compass to find a special side canyon or a particular campsite.

Most of the third edition of this book, like the first and second, is devoted to teaching the fundamentals of navigating with map, compass, and altimeter. In fact, I've written most of the book as if you didn't have a GPS receiver available to you. The third edition would not have been complete, however, without dramatically expanding the chapter on GPS receivers. I'll take a close look at the latest GPS units, with their detailed, built-in maps and sophisticated route-creation and tracking capabilities, and show you how they can interface with maps on your desktop computer to give you still more ways to find your way in the wilderness. GPS receivers today are vastly more capable than the primitive unit I bought in the late 1990s.

Learning the craft of backcountry navigation using all of the available tools gives you the freedom to roam the wilderness at will in any season. Navigation skills, particularly the ability to read a map, also buy you a ticket to hours of mind travel: poring over possible routes and wondering what secrets some serpentine desert canyon holds, what fish might inhabit some lake lost in the wilderness far from any trail, or what elegant climbs might be possible on some sharp-edged ridge or daunting granite face. I still carry a book to read during idle hours, stormbound in camp, but I rarely crack it open. Instead I spend my free time poring over my maps, studying the way the contours lie and the streams run, memorizing the names of prominent peaks and lakes, and planning my next adventure. With maps and your imagination, the world is your playground.

After reading this book, you'll know how to:

- Create a mental image of a landscape while studying a map;

- Use paper maps and computerized mapping tools to help plan your next adventure;

- Use a compass to find your way to a destination and back again;

- Combine map-reading and compass skills to identify a landmark, plot your course, and determine your location;

- Use an altimeter to pinpoint your position;

- Use a GPS receiver to navigate a course from one waypoint to the next, then find your way back home again;

- Avoid the most common route-finding errors;

- Use a whole array of easy navigation tricks that simplify staying found in the wilderness.

My father gave me my first compass when I was twelve, and I've been practicing getting lost with it ever since. Actually, to paraphrase Daniel Boone, I've never really been lost; I've just been mighty confused. After forty-two years of getting confused in far-flung wildernesses from Alaska to Argentina, I've learned route-finding the hard way. If you read this book carefully and (even more important) spend a few hours practicing the skills it teaches, you'll master route-finding the easy way and save yourself a thousand anxious moments in the process.

How to Read a Topographic Map

Sometimes you can solve your navigational problems with just a good map and common sense.

A case in point: Many years ago a friend and I were sea-kayaking along the storm-wracked coast of Alaska's Kenai Fjords National Park. We had just rounded Cape Aialik and were midway through a 20-mile stretch of coastline so consistently walled with cliffs that no landing was possible. Cold rain fell intermittently from the swollen clouds only 100 feet overhead. As we headed north from the cape, we stared hard through the fog, eager to identify Porcupine Cove, the first possible landing site.

In the fog, however, all coves looked alike.

"Is that it?" Bill asked an hour after we rounded the cape. He pointed ahead to an apparent indentation in the coast that seemed, in the fog, to have all the credibility of a mirage. I had to agree that the cove looked vaguely right. I'd examined it carefully when we passed it on our way out a week earlier. Then Bill pulled out the map to double-check. "That can't be it," he decided.

How did he reach that conclusion so quickly? In the fog we could only guess at the cove's outline and dimensions. Although we had been able to see snatches of the coastline as we paddled north, no other landmarks were now visible.

But Bill had landmarks in his head.

"We've only passed two coves so far," he said. "This is the third. Porcupine Cove is still several miles ahead."

That kind of navigating requires no great map-reading skills. It doesn't even demand use of a compass. What it does require is paying careful attention to the landscape around you. Raise your eyes from the ground (or sea) 5 feet ahead and really study your surroundings! That's the first key to successful navigating. Don't be like the frustrated hiker I met last fall who had missed the turnoff to the Mt. Elbert trail and hiked miles out of his way. As he launched into a tirade against the forest service, as if it was responsible for his misfortune, I decided it would just add insult to injury if I pointed out that the sign marking the turnoff was 5 feet high and positioned right next to the trail.

Being aware means looking back over your shoulder as well as forward. The world looks very different heading down the trail than it did heading up. Memorize the shape of the little pinnacle that marks the point where you joined the ridge. Remember the appearance of the fallen logs that mark where the trail turns away from the sandy desert wash. You can't count on your footprints to guide you when you return along the same trail. A group of hikers could come along, miss the junction, and walk half a mile up the wash before realizing their mistake. If you follow the main body of footprints—theirs—you'll make the same error. Even the simplest backcountry errand can become scary if you don't pay attention to the way back. While backpacking in Colorado's Weminuche Wilderness, my brother-in-law, a novice backpacker, volunteered to walk down to the stream a few hundred yards away to filter water. By the time he finished, darkness had fallen. Although he had a headlamp, he still couldn't relocate our campsite hidden in the trees. Fortunately I heard him call my name. I called back, and he quickly relocated the campsite.

Paying attention to your watch can also help you estimate your position. A simple calculation during our attempt to identify the mystery cove would have confirmed Bill's conclusion. We'd only been paddling north from the cape for an hour. We knew from keeping track of hours and miles during the previous week that our average pace was about 3 miles an hour. Without measuring anything, we could have eyeballed the map and seen that we couldn't possibly have paddled from Cape Aialik to Porcupine Cove in just an hour.

Map Basics

In Kenai Fjords a planimetric map would have been adequate. Planimetric maps show the world as if it were all on one plane. A gas station road map is a good example. The map always shows the ground as if the observer was directly overhead. That means a right angle on the ground (a road junction, for example) is always represented by a right angle on the map.

Equally important, 1 inch on the map always represents a particular distance on the ground. That relationship is the map's *scale*. On a map of the United States, the scale might be 1 inch to every 200 miles. On a map useful for hiking, the scale might be 1 inch to every mile or three-eighths of a mile. The scale is usually expressed as a ratio, 1:24,000, for example, which means 1 inch on the map equals 24,000 inches on the ground. Don't worry—you don't need to figure out what fraction of a mile equals 24,000 inches. As I'll explain in more detail later, most maps have a scale diagram that shows graphically what distance on the map equals 1 mile on the ground.

Planimetric maps, like most maps, also have a legend: a chart showing what the symbols used on the map mean. Some symbols are obvious: Irregular blue splotches are typically lakes, for example. Others, like a dashed line, can mean a four-wheel-drive jeep road on one map and a trail for hikers only on another. Knowing the symbol's meaning can help you avoid eating road dust for lunch.

How to Read a Topographic Map

Most interesting wilderness areas are not flat. For them you need a topographic map, called a "topo" for short.

Topographic maps show the ups and downs of the terrain by means of *contour lines.* A contour line is a line on the map that represents the same elevation throughout its length. It may duck into canyons and bulge out around ridges, but it still marks the same elevation. The line indicating the boundary of a lake is a good example of a contour line. To "walk a contour" means to traverse across a slope without gaining or losing elevation.

The easiest way to visualize how contour lines relate to mountains and valleys is to build a little mountain. You'll find the materials in the form of figure 1-1.

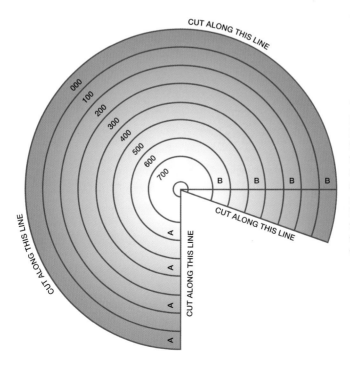

1-1 Cut along the marked lines, place line A over line B, and tape securely. Set the cone you've just made point-up on a tabletop. If you'd rather leave the book intact, photocopy or trace the drawing, then cut out the figure.

First, cut along the outer edge of the figure, as indicated. Place line A atop line B, tape securely, and put the resulting paper cone point-up on a tabletop. Looked at from the side, it should resemble a little volcano with horizontal lines—contour lines—running across it. Each line is at the same height above sea level throughout its length. The elevation change from one line to the next is called the *contour interval.* On any given map it's always the same.

Look at the cone from directly above, as if you were in an airplane flying overhead. Notice how the contour lines form concentric circles. The biggest circle is closest to the tabletop. Successively smaller circles represent higher elevations. This view from above shows your paper volcano in exactly the same way that a topo map would depict it. Figure 1-2 shows how your cone would be mapped.

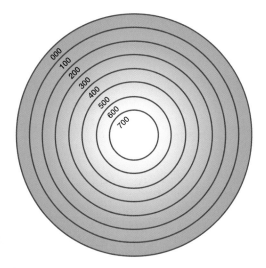

1-2 **Representation of your paper cone on a topographic map.**

That's the first principle of understanding topo maps: Concentric contour lines that form complete, closed paths, whether those paths constitute circles or some irregular shape, represent mountains and hills. Actually, there's one uncommon exception. Circular or semicircular depressions in the earth are represented by similar-looking contours. To distinguish holes from mountains, mapmakers draw

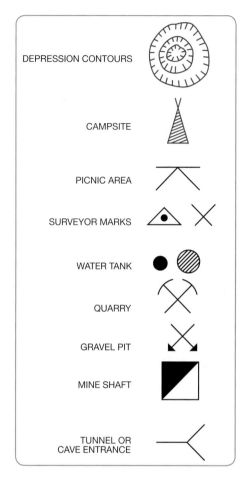

DEPRESSION CONTOURS

CAMPSITE

PICNIC AREA

SURVEYOR MARKS

WATER TANK

QUARRY

GRAVEL PIT

MINE SHAFT

TUNNEL OR
CAVE ENTRANCE

1-3 A selection of topographic map symbols. For a complete listing see the USGS folder "Topographic Maps." You can download a copy as a PDF at http://egsc.usgs. gov/isb/pubs/booklets/symbols/topomapsymbols.pdf.

stubby lines perpendicular to the contours that point to the center of the depression. You can see an example in the list of map symbols in figure 1-3.

To understand how contour lines relate to valleys, look at your paper cone again. Press in slowly on one side of the cone near the bottom to create a valley. Crease the paper so the crease runs along the valley bottom. Now look down at the cone from directly overhead. Let it flatten out in your mind's eye, as if you were looking down at a map. Closing one eye may help. Notice how the contours in the valley form V's whose sharp tips point to higher elevations. Figure 1-4 shows how your volcano-with-valley would be mapped.

That's the second principle of understanding topo maps: Contour lines in valleys form V's pointing to higher ground. Sometimes the V's are softened into U's, but the principle still holds. Ridge contours resemble valley contours except that the contour lines generally form U's and always point to *lower* elevations. On figure 1-4 arrows mark the broad ridges that enclose the valley. The presence of a blue line indicating a stream is a sure sign of a valley, but not all valleys have streams. To be certain whether a group of contours represents a valley or a ridge, you need to look for the elevations marked on the map to determine which way the land is sloping.

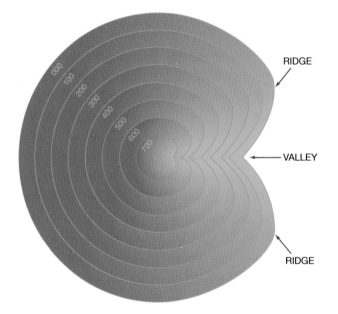

1-4 A topographic-map representation of your paper cone after you crease it to make a valley.

Look at figure 1-5. The thin contour lines are called *intermediate contours*. The darker, thicker contour lines are called *index contours*. Every fifth contour is an index contour. Index contours have the elevation they represent written on them at intervals along their length. Elevations always refer to elevations above mean sea level (the level of the sea averaged over many years and many tidal cycles). To determine which way the ground is sloping at a particular place, locate the two nearest index contours and trace them along until you come to their elevations. Once you know which way the ground is sloping, you can tell whether the bunch of U's or V's you're looking at represent a ridge or a valley.

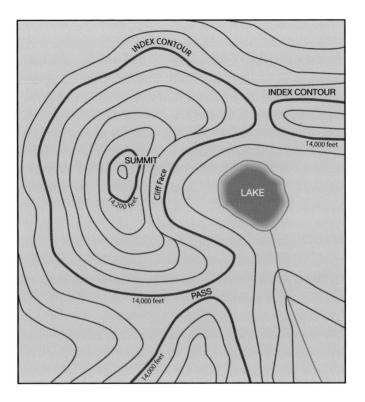

1-5 Thin contour lines are called intermediate contours. Darker contour lines are called index contours. Cliffs and passes are indicated as shown.

Very often you'll see the tips of the U's of two ridges pointing to each other. There are two examples in figure 1-5. This configuration of contour lines represents a pass or saddle. If you started high on either end of the ridge and walked downhill in the direction the contour U's were pointing, you'd end up at the pass—the lowest point along that section of ridge.

The difference in elevation between intermediate contours—the contour interval—is always the same on any particular map. On a map showing hiking trails in Florida, the contour interval might be 10 feet; in the Alaska Range it might be 100 feet. The typical contour interval in the Lower 48 in mountainous terrain is 40 feet. Likewise, the elevation difference between index contours is also constant. It's always equal to five times the contour interval, assuming that your mapmaker, like most, made every fifth contour line an index contour.

Whether the contour interval is 10 feet or 100, the third topo-map principle still applies: The more closely the contours are spaced, the steeper the terrain. That's because the denser the contours, the greater the elevation change over the same horizontal distance. A vertical cliff is the most extreme example: a large elevation change over zero horizontal distance. Mapmakers depict cliffs by drawing contour lines that merge. Figure 1-5 has an example. Another principle: Regardless of the terrain's steepness, a path straight up a slope will always be represented on a map by a straight line perpendicular to the contour lines. Or, to put it the way a skier or snowboarder might, the "fall line," the line straight down a ski slope, would always be drawn on a map as a line that forms a right angle with each contour.

Map Series

In the United States the US Geological Survey is the prime source for paper topographic maps. Although many private companies publish maps in both printed and electronic form, they all use data from the USGS as a primary source for their products.

The USGS publishes many different *series* of maps, each covering a different amount of land. Those most useful to wilderness travelers are the 7.5 minute and 15 minute series. No, a 7.5 minute map doesn't cover the amount of land you can cross in 7.5 minutes, nor does it take 15 minutes to figure out where you are on a 15 minute map. "Minutes," in this case, refers to minutes of latitude and longitude. Sixty minutes makes 1 degree. A 15 minute map, therefore, always covers one-quarter of a degree of latitude and longitude. It takes four 7.5 minute maps to cover the area of one 15 minute map. Both 15 minute and 7.5 minute maps are often called *quadrangles,* or *quads* for short.

Lines of latitude are lines circling the globe parallel to the equator. They're called, logically enough, parallels. One degree of latitude always equals 69 miles. Lines of longitude, called meridians, pass through the poles and form 90-degree angles with the equator. The distance between lines of longitude varies from about 67 miles at the equator to zero to the poles, where all longitude lines converge. In my home state of Colorado, a 7.5 minute map covers an area approximately 8.6 by 6.7 miles.

The area covered by the map—its *series*—does not dictate that any particular *scale* be used. However, the USGS has established some conventions about what scales will be used in each map series. All 7.5 minute maps, for example, use 1:20,000, 1:24,000, or 1:25,000. The 1:20,000 scale is used only in Puerto Rico. All 1:24,000-scale maps give elevations and distances in miles and feet. All 1:25,000-scale maps use metric units. Most 7.5 minute maps use 1:24,000, in which 1 inch equals 2,000 feet or about three-eighths of a mile.

All 15 minute series maps now use the 1:63,360 scale, in which 1 inch equals 1 mile. These maps cover 15 minutes of latitude and 20 to 36 minutes of longitude. Only 15 minute series maps are available for most of Alaska. At present only some areas around Anchorage, Fairbanks, and Prudhoe Bay are mapped at the 1:24,000 scale.

The USGS also makes maps that cover much larger areas, up to and including the entire United States. Confusingly, however, these map series are not designated by the area covered in minutes or degrees but by the scale, such as 1:100,000 or 1:250,000.

While we're on the matter of scale, let's get one other bit of terminology straight: *small-scale* versus *large-scale*. On a small-scale map, landscape features are shown relatively small. On a 1:250,000-scale map, for example (which uses a relatively small scale), a mile-long meadow occupies only a quarter of an inch. On a large-scale map, such as a 7.5 minute, 1:24,000-scale quad, landscape features are shown relatively large. That same mile-long meadow occupies 2⅝ inches. Figure 1-6 summarizes how much territory the different series of maps cover in relation to the state of Colorado. The 1:250,000-series labeled "Denver," for example, covers about one-sixteenth of the state—an area of approximately 3,500 square miles. That's a map useful for auto travel, not hiking.

It's not important to memorize what 1 inch means in all these different scales. All USGS maps have a scale diagram at the bottom of the map that shows what

1-6 Topographic maps of different scales and series cover different areas in relation to the state of Colorado.

distance on the map equals 1 mile on the land. Before studying a map, check the scale diagram. It will help you visualize the terrain.

Fortunately the USGS is a lot more consistent in its use of colors and symbols than it is in its use of scales in a particular series of maps. Black, for example, always indicates a man-made feature such as a road or building. Blue, logically, denotes water: streams, rivers, lakes, oceans. Brown is used for contour lines. Green indicates vegetation: brushy and forested areas. Red designates major highways. It's also used for the boundaries of units of public land: national park boundaries, for example, or townships and sections of land. Purple indicates features added to the map on the basis of aerial photographs. Purple features have not been field-checked, which means nobody visited the site in person and verified what the aerial photograph appeared to show.

The USGS uses several dozen symbols on its maps to indicate everything from surveyor's benchmarks to standard-gauge multiple-track railroads. Figure 1-3 shows the most important symbols for backcountry travelers. Each USGS map shows the road classification symbols. For a complete listing of map symbols, get the USGS's folder called "Topographic Maps." Download it at http://egsc.usgs.gov/isb/pubs/booklets/symbols/topomapsymbols.pdf.

Topo maps depict unchanging physical features very accurately. But as time passes since the date of printing, some natural features are likely to evolve. A pond, for example, may become a meadow; a glacier may advance or recede. Man-made features are also likely to change. Roads may be upgraded or abandoned. New trails may be added or old ones rerouted. If you're visiting a national park or national forest, you may be able to keep up with that kind of change by obtaining an up-to-date planimetric map from the park or national forest administration. A friendly ranger might also help you update your topo map.

You can buy topo maps directly from the USGS as well as from many outdoor specialty shops. To determine the ones you need, obtain an "Index to Topographic and Other Map Coverage" for the state you're interested in. It's free if you order it from the USGS. Retail stores that stock USGS maps should have a shop copy.

The index is a map of the state that shows every topo map published that covers any part of the state. (Some topos cover more than one state.) Each rectangle on the index represents a topo map. The name of the map and the date of the survey are written within the rectangle. In general the smallest rectangles on the index will be 7.5 minute maps; in Alaska they'll be 1:63,360 maps showing 15 minutes of latitude. You can check by counting the number of rectangles between parallels of latitude. If there are eight per degree, the rectangles show 7.5 minute maps because 8 × 7.5 = 60 minutes or 1 degree. Four rectangles per degree means the maps show 15 minutes of latitude. Maps are named for some prominent feature within their boundaries. Often that will help you decide if you need that map. Indexes also show major roads, towns, rivers, and mountains, which may help you to identify which maps you need. When in doubt about a map, order it anyway. Even if your intended route doesn't cross it, you'll probably be looking out at those peaks and valleys when you stop for lunch on the summit. Be sure to specify the state, the quadrangle name, and the map series when ordering. In some cases a 15 minute map may have the same name as a 7.5 minute map contained inside it, which makes the series designation crucial in obtaining the right map.

In Alaska only the 1:250,000 maps have names. The 1:63,360 maps have only letter and number designations. To order a 1:63,360 map, give the name of the 1:250,000 map that contains it, plus the letter and number. An example might be "Fairbanks D-1." If you have a map that covers part of the territory you're interested in, look at its margins. They'll tell you the name of all eight adjoining maps, including those that only touch at one corner. If you don't find the names of the adjacent maps written along the borders, look at the bottom of the map. You'll find a diagram that gives the same information. You can see an example in figure 1-7.

QUADRANGLE LOCATION

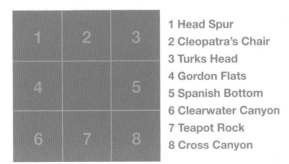

1 Head Spur
2 Cleopatra's Chair
3 Turks Head
4 Gordon Flats
5 Spanish Bottom
6 Clearwater Canyon
7 Teapot Rock
8 Cross Canyon

ADJOINING 7.5 MINUTE QUADRANGLES

1-7 This diagram shows the 7.5 minute quads that adjoin the Elaterite Basin quad, which covers part of Utah's Canyonlands National Park. The Elaterite Basin quad is represented by the empty central square.

You can mail-order US maps directly from the USGS and Canadian maps from the Centre for Topographic Information, a division of Natural Resources Canada; see the contact information in the appendix under Maps.

The Canada map office website provides several ways to locate maps of the region you're interested in. You can display a map of Canada and then click on the region of interest. You can also search by geographic name.

Mail-ordering anything can be tedious, and maps are no exception. Each state index lists all map dealers in the state. You can, of course, also search in your favorite Internet search engine for "map dealers Denver" (or whatever city you're located in). With a little luck, one will be near you. Then you can go and examine maps before buying to be sure you get the right one. Most map dealers carry compasses as well. Many also carry altimeters and GPS receivers.

State indexes also list all the special maps that cover part of the state. In Colorado, for example, Rocky Mountain National Park, Mesa Verde National Park, and Black Canyon of the Gunnison National Park, among other interesting places, all rank special maps of their own. Ordering one of them instead of four or five individual sheets can save you a lot of paperwork when you're out in the field. The disadvantage may be that the scale is smaller.

USGS maps are not the only ones you should consider carrying. Trails Illustrated, a division of National Geographic, offers maps for popular recreation areas in thirty-five states. These maps are printed on a waterproof plastic material, so they're much tougher than a USGS paper map, and they're often more up to date on man-made features like roads and trails—although sometimes they simply repeat errors found on the old USGS quads. When I get particularly frustrated with some egregious error, I refer to the company as "Fables Illustrated."

Usually Trails Illustrated maps will cover the whole region you'll be traveling through on a particular hiking or backpacking trip, making it easier to visualize your entire route. For example, one map may cover all of a particular wilderness area. To do that, the scale must usually be smaller than on a USGS 7.5 minute quad. For example, one commonly used scale on Trails Illustrated maps is 1:40,680, or about 1½ inches to the mile. That's great when you want an overview of the whole area but not ideal for really challenging route-finding, where I find 7.5 minute quads, with their scale of 2⅝ inches to the mile, to be essential. I always carry both kinds of maps, but then again, I'm a map junkie—I already own over 160 7.5 minute quads, and I add to my collection regularly.

Using Maps to Plan Your Trip

Detailed maps are vital in the field, but they're also essential for planning your trip before leaving home. For planning purposes, electronic maps that you can display and manipulate on your home computer are ideal. You can buy maps on CD or download them for a fee. Products from National Geographic, sold under the Trails Illustrated or Topo brand, contain maps at various scales, from an entire state right down to the 7.5 minute USGS quads that are the most detailed available. They also contain the relevant Trails Illustrated maps. Using your mouse, you can draw routes and have the software instantly calculate distance, total elevation gain and loss, as well as net gain or loss. All maintained trails are marked, of course, but not the more technical climbing routes. The routes you draw will snap to nearby trails if the map view you've chosen is one of the Trails Illustrated maps. You can add notes, complete with photos, that optionally include the exact location and elevation of the note. And you can save maps with the routes and notes you've created.

GPS receivers merit an entire chapter of their own, but I'll briefly mention here how computerized maps interact with them. For starters, you can create GPS waypoints simply by clicking on the map. You can then upload those waypoints directly to your receiver. This is vastly easier than adding waypoints to your receiver by measuring the UTM coordinates of each waypoint on a paper map, then punching all fifteen digits for each waypoint into your receiver. You can also download waypoints and tracks to your computer and save them. That way you can delete unneeded waypoints and routes from your receiver without losing them permanently and then upload only those you need for a particular trip, so you're not wading through dozens of irrelevant choices trying to find the correct waypoint for the next leg of your journey.

You can even connect your GPS receiver to a copy of your mapping software running on a laptop and have the software display your position on the map in real time. This could be useful if you were trying to locate a trailhead, for example. Don't try to do this while driving! Pull over and check the map, or better yet, have a passenger handle the navigation chores.

I'll explain the relationship between computerized maps, paper maps, and GPS receivers in more detail in Chapter 7, but there is one potential pitfall I'll mention here. USGS maps, and the maps derived from them, are all based on a particular coordinate system called a datum. The datum specifies both a reference point from which measurements within the coordinate system are made and, often, a mathematical model of the shape of the Earth. The datum each map uses is printed in the lower-left corner. Many USGS 7.5 minute quads use NAD 27, which is short for North American Datum 1927. Computerized maps may by default use NAD

83, the North American Datum 1983, or WGS 84 (World Geodetic System 1984), which is essentially identical to NAD 83. Many GPS receivers use WGS 84 by default.

To avoid confusing yourself, be sure that the map datum you set in your mapping software and on your GPS receiver is the same as the map datum used by your paper topographic map. If you don't, the waypoints you create in your mapping software, then transfer to your GPS receiver, and finally try to plot on your paper map may be off by several hundred yards. The problem becomes most obvious if you try to plot a position fix given by your GPS receiver onto a map with a different datum. In a worst-case scenario, your true position may be south of your tent, but when you plot your location on your map, it shows you that you're north of your tent. That kind of error could be serious if you're trying to relocate your tent at night or in a blizzard.

As a planning tool, a computerized map is hard to beat, but it does have one big limitation. While you can print maps, you're limited to printing maps no bigger than your printer can handle—normally 8½ × 11. If you print the map at a scale of 1:24,000, the standard scale on 7.5 minute USGS quads, the map only covers an area measuring 3 × 4 miles. You can print at a smaller scale, of course, which will include more area, but then you may not have the detail you need for tough route-finding. I love computerized maps for planning purposes, but I always carry full-size maps from the USGS and Trails Illustrated when I'm in the field.

Calculating Distance and Travel Time in the Field

Planning your trip in advance is always essential, but what if you change your mind about your route once you get in the field? You'll want to be able to calculate travel time on the fly. And even more important, you'll want to know if it's feasible to take the route you're contemplating.

If a maintained trail leads to your destination, then all you need to know is the time required. That is primarily controlled by two factors: horizontal distance and elevation gain or loss.

First, calculate the horizontal distance. A ruler makes it easy to measure the straight-line distance, but trails never run straight. In fact, they're notorious for taking a lot more miles to reach a destination than the straight-line distance would indicate. The low-tech way to calculate distance along a trail is to use a bit of nonelastic string or a pipe cleaner. Place one end of the string on the trailhead, and then trace the trail with the string, following the trail as it twists and turns. Use your thumbnail to mark the point where the string crosses your destination; then bring the string down to the scale at the bottom of the map and read off the distance. If your route is longer than the scale is long, you'll need to measure the string in scale-length chunks. It's a good idea to add a pessimism factor of 10 or 20 percent to account for the curves you shortcut and the switchbacks the mapmaker neglected to show.

As an alternative measuring tool, use the edge of your compass. One edge on many models is marked in inches. Use short, straight distances to approximate curves.

The most accurate way to measure distances on a map in the field is with a map-measuring device. The most common ones have a wheel that you roll along the map surface. A pointer or digital readout indicates miles or kilometers for several different map scales. Currently, the best ones available are made by the Scalex Corporation. Of course they're also the heaviest, bulkiest, and most expensive. (What, were you expecting a miracle or something?) My Scalex MapWheel is about the size of a large digital fever thermometer; it weighs 2.3 ounces without case, 5.2 ounces with. The MapWheel is an electronic tool that is already programmed with most standard map scales. You can also create and save custom scales, a highly useful feature for measuring distances on Trails Illustrated topos, which have nonstandard scales. All of these measuring methods are easiest to do on a flat surface, like your tent floor before you strike camp. (Okay, I've been in some of *those* campsites, too, but you get my point.)

After determining the mileage, calculate the elevation change. First, determine your starting elevation. Find the index contour closest to your location, and trace along it until you find a place where the map gives its elevation. Then count the number of intermediate contours between your index contour and your location. Multiply the number of intermediate contours by the contour interval (it's given at the bottom of the map) and add that number to (or subtract it from) the elevation of the index contour. For example, let's say the closest index contour is below your location. It reads 10,000 feet. The contour interval is 40 feet, and your location is three contours above the 10,000-foot index contour. You're at 10,120 feet (3 × 40 = 120; 10,000 + 120 = 10,120 feet). Similarly, if the closest index contour is above your location, count the number of intermediate contours between the index contour and your location, multiply by the contour interval, and subtract that total from the index contour to get your elevation.

Determine the elevation of your destination the same way. Subtract, and you have your elevation gain or loss.

In some cases you may find that the map doesn't give an elevation for the index contour closest to your location. In that case find the nearest index contour that does have an elevation indicated, and then calculate the elevation of the index contour near the trailhead. If every fifth contour is an index contour, as is normal, then the elevation difference between index contours equals five times the contour interval. For example, if the contour interval is 40 feet and every fifth contour is an index contour, then the elevation change between index contours is 200 feet.

If the trail runs up and down, be sure to add up all the individual segments of elevation gain and loss.

Now you have the most important information for estimating travel time: distance and elevation gain. But there are other variables as well: your fitness, your load, the altitude, the roughness of the trail, the depth of snow (if any), your mode of transportation (foot, skis, or snowshoes), and whether you're out for the exercise or to admire wildlife. Two miles an hour is a reasonable pace on a level trail with a moderate load. For every 1,000 feet of elevation gain, add an hour to the time you calculated for the mileage alone. That'll give you a very rough estimate. Then hit the trails! Write down your times over different kinds of terrain. Make sure you add in rest stops. It's been my habit for years to record in a journal just how long it actually took me to travel from point A to point B. That gives me a good reality check when I start planning my next trip to the same area. You'll soon learn what's reasonable for you.

If no trail leads to your destination, getting there by any route may be problematical. Your map can give you important clues to the easiest route, but only an actual visit—or a call to a knowledgeable local—will tell you if your planned route is feasible. Those green areas, for example, may be open woods allowing pleasant strolling; they may also be nearly impenetrable thickets of alder, willow, and devil's club. The most important information the map gives to those planning an off-trail hike is probably the average angle of the steepest part of the route.

Find your route's steepest part by locating the place where the contours are closest together. Then measure that horizontal distance. USGS maps have scales in both miles and feet. In this case use the feet scale because you'll be determining the elevation in feet.

Next, calculate the vertical rise over that same horizontal distance.

If the vertical rise is the same as the horizontal distance, you're looking at a 45-degree slope that probably involves stiff scrambling, and it may confront you with some real cliffs. If the vertical rise is greater than the horizontal distance, you're most likely confronting mountaineering territory where you'd be well advised to have a rope, some hardware, and some well-honed climbing skills.

When the rise is only half the horizontal distance, you're looking at a slope of 27 degrees—steep hiking, but only hiking. You can probably find your way around any clifflets that may be hiding in between the contour lines.

To estimate the angle of a slope on a USGS 7.5 minute topographic map with a contour interval of 40 feet, measure the distance between two index contours (the dark lines drawn as every fifth contour). Most compasses have a ruler inscribed along the edge, which makes it easy to measure the distance in the field. For some compasses the units are millimeters; for others, tenths of an inch or other fractions of an inch. Take that measurement to the appropriate chart shown in figure 1-8 to determine the slope angle.

Fig. 1-8 Slope Angle Chart	
Distance between index contours on a 7.5 minute USGS quad (40-foot contour interval) in tenths of an inch	**Slope angle**
0.1	45 degrees
0.15	34 degrees
0.2	27 degrees
0.25	22 degrees
0.3	18 degrees
Distance between index contours on a 7.5 minute USGS quad (40-foot contour interval) in fractions of an inch	**Slope angle**
1/16	58 degrees
1/8	39 degrees
3/16	28 degrees
1/4	22 degrees
5/16	18 degrees
Distance between index contours on a 7.5 minute USGS quad (40-foot contour interval) in millimeters	**Slope angle**
2	52 degrees
3	40 degrees
4	32 degrees
5	27 degrees
6	23 degrees
7	20 degrees
8	18 degrees

1-8. This chart shows the angle of slope for different distances between index contours on a USGS 7.5 minute quad with a 40-foot contour interval.

Savvy winter travelers know that most avalanches run on slopes between 30 and 45 degrees. By measuring the distance between the closest-together index contours along your route, you can get a quick assessment of possible avalanche danger. Be wary of 30- to 45-degree slopes that rise above you, even if you yourself are on lower-angle terrain. My compass has a scale in tenths of an inch, so I printed that portion of the chart on an adhesive address label and attached the label to the inside of the lid of my mirror-sight compass so it would be as handy as possible.

Like all generalizations, there are exceptions to these rules of thumb about slope angles. In the canyon country of the American Southwest, for example, certain geological strata routinely form cliffs. The average angle of the slope climbing out of a canyon may be quite moderate, but the steepest angle is often vertical. Short but impassable cliffs can run for miles without a navigable break. The same is true in parts of the Canadian Rockies and Colorado's San Juans. These cliffs may not be marked as cliffs on the map because they aren't tall enough to span several contours. Once again, local experience is the real key.

How long will a cross-country route take? If you're bushwhacking or scrambling amidst cliff bands, the time required is anyone's guess. It could take two, three, four hours or more to travel a mile. On the other hand, if you're strolling along a smooth, level ridge above timberline, a mile might take you only half an hour.

If your route combines trail walking and cross-country travel, you'll usually save time if you stick to the trail until you're as close as possible to your destination, then head straight for it. Leaving the trail when you first catch sight of the peak you want to climb and heading diagonally up a steep slope usually takes longer than walking the trail until you're directly below the summit.

Winter, of course, adds yet another variable to the mix. If I'm traveling on snowshoes, particularly if I'm breaking trail, I assume my pace will be about half of what it was in the summer even if I can stay on the route taken by the summer trail. If I'm breaking trail *and* bushwhacking through the woods, my pace slows still further. Regardless of the season, you'll need to spend some time in the country to learn how the map features translate into terrain and how far you can actually travel in an hour or a day.

Choosing and Using a Compass

A vicious squall was raking the treeless tundra below Alaska's Mt. Sanford. Snow driven by a 40-mph gale blew horizontally past the cabin windows. The quarter-inch-thick guy wires supporting the cabin whistled and shrieked as the wind dealt body blows to the flimsy plywood walls. Visibility—between the gusts—sometimes reached 50 yards. Somewhere out in the maelstrom, Chris Haaland and Sara Ballantyne were carrying a load of mountaineering gear toward the foot of Sanford's Sheep Glacier.

Only rolling brown hills dissected by wandering streams lay between the cabin and the glacier. All looked identical, particularly when viewed through ice-encrusted lashes and a punishing veil of flying snow. To make the route-finding even more difficult, Chris and Sarah planned to return to the cabin that evening, after caching their equipment.

But Chris and Sara had one thing going for them. They knew approximately where the cabin was on the map and where they wanted to go. Based on that knowledge, they had taken a course off the map. In other words, they had used a compass to measure the angle between true north and the direction they needed to travel.

As soon as they stepped from the cabin, they sighted along their course as far as they could see, picked a landmark, and headed in that direction. Whenever they reached a high point—a ridge or hilltop—they built a small pile of stones, called a cairn, to aid their return.* Then they sighted along their course again, picked another landmark, and continued.

Eventually they felt rather than saw that they had reached a low pass. Below them lay Sheep Glacier. They cached their loads, turned around, and began following their cairns toward home. Without the cairns to correct their course periodically in the rough terrain, they might well have wandered away from their

---

*Cairns should be used only when absolutely necessary and should be knocked down and scattered during your return trip so that no evidence remains of your passage.

route without realizing it. At dusk, with the storm still pounding the tundra outside, they walked into the welcome shelter of the cabin.

Chris and Sara had navigated across 6½ miles of tundra—and back—using nothing but a compass, a few piles of rocks, and an initial course taken off the map. Once the storm closed in, the map was of little further use. If they had had even a few minutes' visibility before the squalls blew in—just long enough to take a compass bearing off their destination—they wouldn't even have needed the map. Ingenuity and a compass are often enough by themselves to find your way.

Contrast Chris and Sara's adroit use of a compass in foul weather with that of a group of seven experienced skiers near Aspen some winters back. Caught in a whiteout above timberline by a fierce snowstorm and unable to find their destination, a backcountry ski hut, the entire group bivouacked in an open pit with no tent and with sleeping bags designed for the 50-degree warmth of a cabin, not the near-zero cold of a February night in the high country. The next day the group splintered into three contingents. One pair of skiers did successfully navigate through the storm back to the trailhead where they had parked on the north side of the range and escaped unharmed. The other two groups, however, both failed to pull out their compasses at a critical juncture and ended up going south instead of north. The pair of lost skiers spent another night in the open before finding a cabin, while the trio of wayward adventurers endured an additional two nights outdoors before finding shelter. Four of the lost skiers suffered frostbite, two quite seriously, before they were rescued.

In retrospect, it's easy to point out the many mistakes the lost Aspen skiers made. But there is also an important lesson to be learned: It is at those times when panic is baying at your heels and every instinct you have is commanding you to plunge ahead heedlessly that you most need to slow down, pull out your compass, take a deep breath, and navigate carefully to your destination.

Compass Basics

The most basic compass is simply a magnetic needle suspended on a pivot so that the needle can align itself with the Earth's magnetic field. The needle is usually mounted in some kind of circular housing marked with the cardinal directions: north, south, east, and west. Although even the simplest compass lets you roughly determine directions, for precise navigation you need something more sophisticated.

First, you need a compass that lets you sight some landmark in the field and take its *bearing*. A bearing is nothing more than the *angle* between a line heading north from your position and a line heading toward the landmark. (The north line

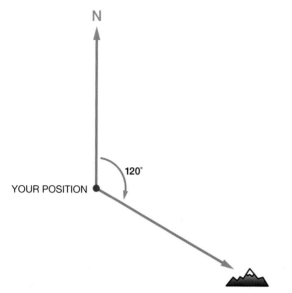

2-1 Bearings are angles measured clockwise from north. North can be defined as true north or magnetic north. The bearing of the mountain is 120 degrees.

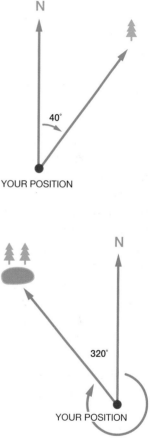

can be defined as either true north, the direction of the North Pole, or magnetic north, the direction the compass needle points. I'll get into that difference later.) For now, study figure 2-1 and memorize this concept: A bearing is an angle, measured in degrees, between a line heading north and a line heading toward your landmark. You always start counting at the north line, and you always count *clockwise* around the compass dial.

Second, you need a compass that lets you measure angles on a map. Once again, the angle of interest will be between a line running north and a line running through your position and some mapped landmark. I'll call that angle a *course,* since you will normally use that angle to pick the course you will travel. For that purpose the compass *needle* is unnecessary. What you really want is a *protractor:* a device for measuring angles.

2-1 cont. The bearing of the tree is 40 degrees.

2-1 cont. The bearing of the lake is 320 degrees—not 40 degrees. (Always measure clockwise around the scale from north.)

Since it's awkward to carry around both a compass and a protractor, compass manufacturers have combined the two instruments into one. They're called *protractor compasses,* or, more commonly, *baseplate compasses,* and they're fundamental to most of the navigational techniques discussed in this book. Figure 2-2 shows their basic parts.

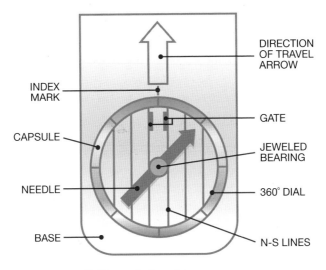

2-2 Parts of a baseplate compass.

The baseplate compass is named for its clear rectangular base. The circular housing for the compass needle is mounted at one end of this rectangular base. Let's call that circular housing the *capsule.* The capsule rotates in relation to the baseplate. The outer edge of the capsule is marked "north," "south," "east," and "west" and is also marked in degrees, increasing as you move around the capsule clockwise. Zero degrees equals north; 90 degrees equals east; 180 degrees equals south; 270 degrees equals west; and 360 degrees once again equals north, or zero. Inside the capsule you'll usually see a series of parallel lines. They're called *north-south lines* because they lie parallel to a line running through the north and south points on the capsule.

Most baseplate compasses have an arrow inscribed on the base. It's called the *direction-of-travel arrow* because it indicates the direction you want to go when the capsule is set to a course you've taken off the map. You point the same arrow at a landmark in the field when you want to measure a bearing. The foot of the direction-of-travel arrow serves as the *index mark* where you read off the number of degrees to which the capsule is set. To set the capsule to any angle between zero and 360 degrees, turn the capsule until the correct number of degrees is aligned with the index mark.

The compass needle rotates within the capsule, coming to rest when the north end of the needle points to magnetic north. Many map-and-compass operations require you to twist the capsule until the north end of the needle points to the north mark on the capsule. To make it easy to determine when the needle and the capsule's north mark are accurately aligned, the capsule has a long, thin rectangle or box inscribed on its bottom surface. I'll call that rectangle the *gate*. Later in this book, when I say, "Place the needle in the gate," I mean to align the needle so it lies entirely inside the gate and so its north end points to the northern end of the gate, which is usually marked in red.

Together those three moving parts—baseplate, capsule, and needle—let you measure the bearing of a landmark in the field and measure courses on the map. I'll tell you how after I finish discussing compasses.

Some baseplate compasses have a mirror attached to the baseplate with a hinge (figure 2-3). When you're taking a bearing, that mirror lets you see both the object you're sighting and the capsule at the same time. Using the mirror significantly increases the accuracy of your bearing measurement compared to just

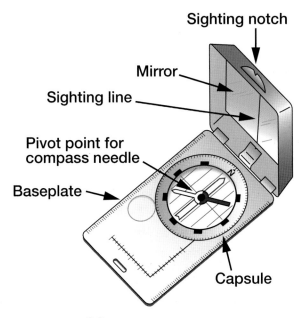

2-3 A mirror-sight compass.

holding the compass in your hand at waist level and trying to point the direction-of-travel arrow at the object you're sighting. The mirror also lets you admire your handsomely weather-beaten features after a week in the backcountry—greasy hair, burnt cheeks, and all. More importantly, the mirror can also be used as an emergency signaling device. For the first and third reasons only, I recommend a mirror-sighting model. I'll explain in detail how to use a mirror-sight compass later in this chapter.

As I've already mentioned, compass needles almost never point to true north. The difference in direction between *true north* and *magnetic north* is an angle called the *declination*. All USGS maps state in the bottom margin the declination for the region covered by the map. Compensating for the difference between magnetic and true north when doing map-and-compass work with a standard baseplate compass requires some simple addition and subtraction. When you take a bearing in the field, you've measured an angle between magnetic north, indicated by the compass needle, and your landmark. When you take a course off a map, however, you've measured an angle between true north, indicated by the top of the map, and your landmark. You have to reconcile the different starting points for your measurements, a process I'll describe in the next chapter.

If you'd rather not mess with that, you can buy a "set-and-forget" compass that lets you set the declination and forget about it until you travel to a different area of the country. Let me explain.

On standard baseplate compasses the gate marked on the capsule is fixed in relation to the capsule. When you place the north end of the needle in the north part of the gate, the needle points exactly at the north mark on the capsule.

Set-and-forget compasses, on the other hand, have a gate that moves in relation to the north mark on the capsule. You set that moveable gate at an angle to true north equal to the declination and forget about it until you travel to some different region, where the declination is different. Now when you place the needle in the gate, the needle points to magnetic north and the north mark on the capsule points to true north. See figure 2-4. There's no need to do any addition or subtraction, or even to remember what the declination equals. Set-and-forget compasses are indeed much easier to use, and I strongly recommend them.

Every compass worth buying will be fluid-dampened. That means a fluid within the capsule prevents the needle from swinging to and fro like a hypnotist's watch. Good compasses will still function at −40 degrees F, although it's best to keep the compass inside your coat to prevent bubbles from forming as the liquid contracts. High altitude, particularly when combined with severe cold, can also cause a bubble to appear. The bubble won't interfere with accuracy unless it's bigger than a quarter

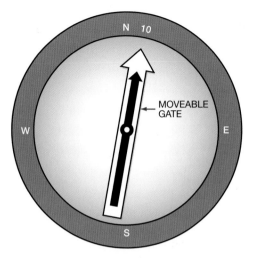

2-4 A set-and-forget compass set for a declination of 10 degrees east. The needle points to magnetic north; the "N" mark on the capsule indicates true north.

inch in diameter. Usually the bubble will disappear when you return to normal temperatures and sea level. If it doesn't, you may have a leak. Avoid buying a compass that already has a large bubble in the capsule.

You should also protect your compass from extreme heat, such as the dashboard of your car. High temperatures cause the liquid to expand, which can rupture the capsule.

Be sure to buy your compass in the region where you intend to use it. Only along a line known as the magnetic equator, which lies near the geographical equator, do compass needles sit level with the Earth's surface. North of the magnetic equator, they dip to the north; south of the magnetic equator, they dip to the south. Manufacturers compensate by counterbalancing the compass needle so that the needle pivots freely when the compass is held horizontally. Silva, for example, makes compasses balanced for five different magnetic zones. If you take a compass balanced correctly for the United States to Australia, the needle is likely to bind when you hold the compass level.

It'll make my job—and yours—a lot easier if you go out and buy yourself a baseplate compass and a topo map before you continue reading this book. There's nothing like having the real thing in your hands to make all this talk of aligning needles in gates and twisting capsules to different bearings seem as simple as it really is. If a picture is worth a thousand words, then actual experience is worth 10,000.

Using a Compass in the Field

Now that you've got a map and compass in your hands, you're about ready to use it. First, though, you need to know about a common pitfall. Dale Atkins, a mission leader for Colorado's Alpine Rescue Group, tells a story that illustrates the point perfectly.

One day several years ago, a group of hunters drove to the trailhead below Mt. Evans, got out of their truck, and spread out their map on the hood. They carefully oriented the map with the compass and just as carefully followed the direction the compass needle said was north. That night, when two teenage members of the group did not return, the adults reported them missing. Dale and a search team from Alpine Rescue drove to the trailhead.

"They went north," the adults said, pointing toward a small peak. Dale walked 30 feet away from the truck and got out his compass.

"But north is that way," he said, pointing in a direction 45 degrees away from the peak. Fortunately Dale's search team found the teenagers unharmed.

The hunters' mistake? Using their compass on the hood of their truck. Any metal object, even much smaller ones like pocket knives and belt buckles, can throw off the compass needle. The same is true of all electronic devices. Any time current flows through a wire, it generates a magnetic field. That field can affect the compass needle.

Before using your compass, therefore, make sure nothing metallic or electronic is affecting it. Once you've done that, trust it. Only once in all my years of compass use have I set my compass down on a rock and found that some metallic ore in the rock was affecting the needle. Simply standing up and walking a few feet freed the needle from the rock's influence.

The first technique to learn is how to take a bearing off a landmark and then walk that bearing. Since you're not, at this time, relating your bearings to a map, there's no need to worry about the difference between true north and magnetic north. You can simply relate all directions to magnetic north.

Let's assume you bought a baseplate compass without a mirror sight. To take a bearing off a landmark in the field, point the direction-of-travel arrow at the landmark. Hold the compass level so the needle can swing freely. Now hold the baseplate still and rotate the capsule until you've put the needle in the gate—in other words, until the north end of the needle points to the north mark on the capsule. Then read the bearing at the index mark. Figure 2-5 shows you how. In this example, the bearing is 316 degrees.

All that you've done is to measure the angle between a line heading toward magnetic north, as indicated by the compass needle, and a line heading toward your landmark, as indicated by the direction-of-travel arrow. The angle is always measured clockwise around the compass dial, starting at north.

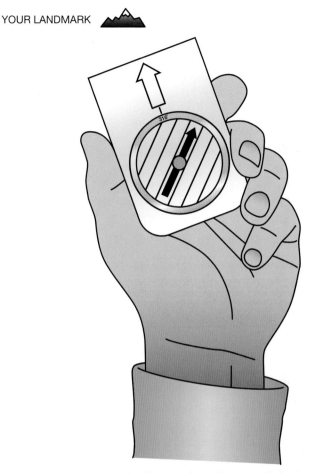

YOUR LANDMARK

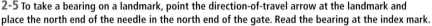

2-5 To take a bearing on a landmark, point the direction-of-travel arrow at the landmark and place the north end of the needle in the north end of the gate. Read the bearing at the index mark.

You can use a mirror-sight compass just like a regular baseplate compass. To do so, open the mirror housing all the way until the compass lies flat. On most models a line will be inscribed on the mirror. It lies parallel to the long edges of the compass and starts at a notch in the center of the cover's top edge. That line serves as the direction-of-travel arrow. Holding the compass at waist level, proceed as you would with a standard compass.

For more accuracy, however, hold the compass level at about the height of your chin. You'll have to adjust that height a bit if you're sighting an object either above or below your position. Now open the mirror cover until you can see the capsule in the mirror. The mirror and baseplate should form an angle of 70 degrees or less. Hold the compass so the line inscribed on the mirror (the sighting line) passes directly through the needle's pivot point as you look at the reflection of the capsule. Doing that ensures that the long edges of the compass point directly at the landmark. Now sight the landmark through the notch in the center of the cover's top edge. Place the needle in the gate by twisting the capsule. Double-check that the sighting line on the mirror is still passing through the needle's pivot point. Read the bearing at the index mark (see figure 2-6).

Now you've got a bearing on your landmark. Let's say that you, like Chris and Sara, want to walk toward this particular landmark. Just after you start, a storm rolls in, so you're forced to navigate by compass. Or perhaps you've climbed to a mountaintop and want to take a different way down. You can see your destination—a lake, let's say—but shortly after you drop off the summit, you'll be in thick woods and the lake will be invisible. You could just start out walking the bearing, figuring you'll get there in an hour or two. But walking in a straight line in rough terrain, when visibility is bad or when there are no directional clues—for example, when hiking through a forest on a cloudy day—is a lot tougher than you'd expect.

In fact, a 2009 study at the Max Planck Institute for Biological Cybernetics in Germany found that hikers traveling through a forest on an overcast day, with no visible sun to orient from, invariably ended up walking in circles. Other subjects attempted to walk across a grassy field while blindfolded. None could walk a straight line, and some subjects ended up walking in circles as small as 66 feet in diameter. Even subjects who felt completely confident that they were heading in the right direction quickly wandered off their desired course, often eventually heading back the way they had come. The study concluded that we simply can't trust our senses to guide us unless we have some visible landmark or a compass to orient us. No one, it seems, actually has "a good sense of direction" built into their head.

That point came home to me dramatically in 1980. It was the morning of our tenth day on Alaska's Mt. Hunter, and we were in deep trouble. Already our ascent had taken three days longer than we expected, and we were still far from home. The mountain's steep ice and steeper rock had sapped our strength, and the frequent storms punctuating the unremitting cold only exacerbated our difficult situation. It was time to get out of there, but the desperate climbing below made it clear we could not descend down the south face. The only way out lay across the summit plateau and down the long and difficult west ridge. The intense cold had frostbitten my fingers, and it was threatening to do the same to Peter Metcalf's and Pete Athens's toes. We could have wolfed our remaining food in a single meal, yet

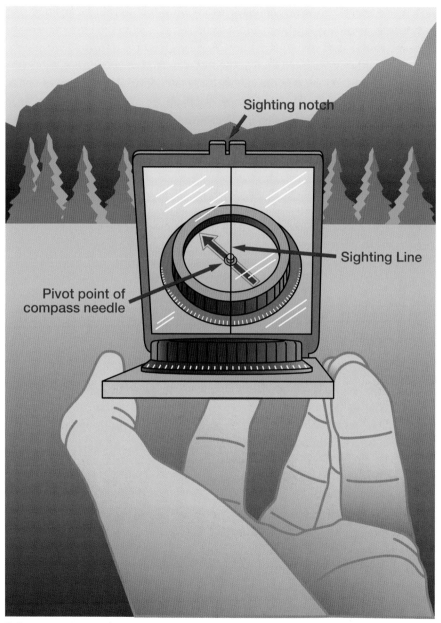

2-6 To take a bearing with a mirror-sight compass, hold the compass level and align the notch at the top of the mirror with the object you're sighting. Position the compass so the sighting line in the middle of the mirror passes through the pivot point for the needle, then twist the capsule until the needle lies within the gate.

we knew it would be many more days before we would eat our fill again. But at least the day had dawned clear, and the first few miles across the summit plateau appeared to be easy.

Shortly after we emerged from our snow cave, our next landmark, the junction of the west ridge and the summit plateau, came into view. We hurried on as fast as the deep snow and our emaciated bodies would permit.

Within an hour clouds boiled up from below and engulfed us in a soundless white void. Like fools, we had neglected to take a compass bearing on our landmark. But at least we could measure a course on the map based on our best estimate of our position. I was leading and Pete Athens was in the rear, trying to keep our three-man rope team heading in the right direction by shouting course corrections.

The storm intensified. Athens shouted to me to turn left 90 degrees—a direction that my instinct told me was 90 degrees wrong. For a minute we tried to argue over the screaming wind. Then I gave up and obeyed the compass.

Three hours later, exhausted, with darkness imminent and our position a mystery, we dug another snow cave. As we chipped wearily at the ice, the storm vanished as quickly as it had come. We bolted from the cave. There, only a quarter of a mile away, shining in the low light of the setting sun, was the junction of the west ridge and the plateau. Without a map and compass, the skill to use them, and at least one cool head to insist we should trust them, we might have wandered on the plateau for another day or longer, worsening our frostbite, hastening the deterioration of our already wasted bodies, and further reducing the chances of descending safely.

A disciplined approach to navigating is all that's required to avoid wandering in circles. Once you've got a bearing on your distant landmark, sight through the compass again, but this time, pick a landmark close at hand. In really foul weather or in the woods, that might mean something only a hundred yards away. Walk to that object, sight again, and pick another landmark at the limit of good visibility. Continue until you reach your destination.

Let's say you encounter some obstacle you can't walk over as you follow your compass bearing. It could be a lake; it could be a stream where you'll have to walk up or down to find a ford or fallen log; it could be a wide crevasse in a glacier or a hill ringed with cliffs. If you can see across the obstacle, the solution is simple. Sight along your bearing to some object on the far side of the obstacle, do whatever you have to do to get around the obstacle, and walk to the object you sighted. Pick another landmark along your former line of travel, and continue.

If you can't see across the obstacle—the fog's too thick, let's say, or you're confronting a cliff—then you'll have to maintain your sense of direction while you skirt the obstacle. First, decide if you want to go around the obstacle to the right or left. Let's say right looks easier. Make a right-angle (90-degree) turn to your right and walk far enough to clear the obstacle. Count your steps as you go. Now turn 90 degrees to your left, which puts you back on your original bearing, and walk until you're sure you've cleared the obstacle. There's no need to count steps here. Make another left-hand 90-degree turn and walk the same number of steps you counted after your first turn. That puts you back on your original line of travel. Turn right, sight a landmark on your original bearing, and proceed. All you've done is walk three sides of a rectangle so that when you arrive on the far side of the obstacle, you're back on your original line of travel. Figure 2-7 makes all this clear.

To simplify making all those 90-degree turns, use the short edges of the baseplate to sight landmarks. To make the initial 90-degree right turn, for example, face in roughly the correct direction and sight along a short edge of the baseplate while keeping the needle in the gate. Pick a landmark and go, counting your steps. When you've cleared the obstacle, make the first left turn by sighting an object along your original bearing, using the compass in the normal way. To make the second left turn, face in roughly the correct direction and sight again along a short edge of the baseplate with the needle in the gate. Pick a landmark, pace out your measured distance, and you're back on track.

To return home, you want to walk in exactly the opposite direction—180 degrees opposite. To do so, you can either add 180 degrees to your original bearing

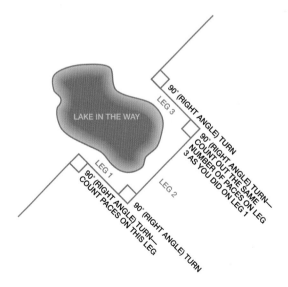

2-7 Maintaining your course while circumventing an obstacle.

or subtract it. Use whatever operation keeps the result between zero and 360. Or you can align the south end of the needle in the north end of the gate on the capsule. Either operation will point you toward home. You then pick landmarks and walk toward them in exactly the same way you did heading out.

All by itself, a compass can often get you to your destination. Add a detailed topographic map, and you've got very few excuses for getting lost. I'll describe how to use the two together in the next chapter.

Using Compass and Map Together

The call was urgent: Two mountaineers were overdue on James Peak. Given the vicious midwinter storm pummeling Colorado's Front Range, overdue probably meant lost and in trouble. The dispatcher for Alpine Rescue, who had received the call, immediately paged all available members.

Dale Atkins met several teammates at the trailhead and formed a search plan. They would begin by climbing St. Mary's Glacier. Then they would head west across the treeless alpine barrens toward the 13,294-foot summit of James Peak. When they finished searching there, they would turn to the north and descend to James Peak Lake. Snowmobiles would meet them at the lake and take them back to the road.

A westerly gale made every step a struggle as they started up St. Mary's Glacier. The unrelenting wind kicked up a ground blizzard that slashed visibility to a few feet. The worst gusts struck like tsunamis, threatening to knock them flat. All the searchers possessed tremendous winter mountaineering experience, however, and were intimately familiar with the James Peak area. There seemed to be no need to fool around with their maps and compasses, which remained securely stowed inside their packs. They completed their search of the region above timberline without locating the missing climbers, turned to the north, and descended to the lake.

No snowmobiles! Surprised, they radioed their dispatcher. The snowmobiles, they were told, were at the lake and waiting. "Where are you guys?" the dispatcher asked.

The search group started walking around the lake. A dam emerged through the flying snow. Suddenly a sickening feeling of recognition flashed into their minds. Somehow they had turned south near the summit, not north, and descended to Loch Lomond, on exactly the wrong side of the mountain. Sheepishly, they walked back to their vehicles. The lost mountaineers hiked out a day later, uninjured. Every winter thereafter Alpine Rescue's members gave the mission leader for that search a roll of bright pink surveyor's tape so he could mark his trail and find his way home.*

As those hapless searchers demonstrated, the best map-and-compass skills in the world are worthless if you don't pull out the tools and use them. It can be really hard to locate your position if the first time you check your map is several hours after you wander away from the last landmark you can identify. It's particularly hard to find yourself if you don't keep track of the direction you're traveling. That sounds obvious, but as Dale and company showed, even the best can get cocky about their ability to navigate without navigational tools.

Orienting the Map—and Yourself

The best place for your first map check is the trailhead. Start by finding your location on the map. Usually that's easy: You're at the end of the road or at the marked point where the trail leaves the highway. Sometimes, though, it's not so obvious, such as when you're starting a cross-country hike. If you haven't parked near some obvious, mapped landmark, you may need to use the more sophisticated techniques I'll describe later to pinpoint your position.

Next, orient the map. In other words, place the map on some flat surface (*not* the hood of your car!) so that directions on the map correspond to directions in the field. It's always easiest to visualize what you're doing if the map is oriented. Sometimes you can orient the map by eye. If there's a lake straight ahead of you and a prominent hill to your right, twist the map until the lake lies straight ahead of your position on the map and the hill is to the right of that position. Here's another way to look at it: A map is oriented correctly if a line drawn from your position on the map to the mapped lake points straight toward the real lake. In similar fashion, all other directions on the map will also correspond to reality.

Sometimes, though, you can't orient by eye. The landscape may lack any obvious mapped features. Or it may have too many features, and you can't tell which is which. In that case you need to use your compass to orient the map.

Here, and for the rest of this chapter, I'm going to assume that magnetic north and true north lie in exactly the same direction. That assumption will make it a lot easier for you to learn. In the next chapter I'll tell you how to compensate for the difference that usually exists between those directions.

---

*Although surveyor's tape can be a valuable tool in some search-and-rescue operations, it should always be removed when the search is concluded to prevent degradation of the land's wilderness character. It should not be used in ordinary route-finding activities.

On almost all maps north is at the top of the sheet. To orient the map roughly, hold the compass horizontally and glance at the needle. It points north, of course; place the map so the top also points north. Note that when the map is oriented correctly, the left and right margins will represent lines running north and south.

To orient the map more accurately, set the capsule to zero degrees. Place the compass on the map so one long edge of the baseplate lies atop either the left or right margin. Now rotate map and compass together as a unit until you've placed the needle in the gate, so the north end of the needle points to the north mark on the capsule. The map is now oriented. Every direction on the map corresponds to directions in reality. Figure 3-1 shows a correctly oriented map.

Now that you've found your position and oriented the map, take a look around and identify some nearby landmarks. Determine your general direction of travel. Does your route run north, south, east, or west? Try to develop a feel for the relationship between the cardinal directions and major terrain features. You might note, for example, that the valley you'll be hiking up runs east and west, while the region's highest peak is basically to the north. Knowing where you started and what direction you're traveling will help prevent dumbness attacks like placing the south end of the compass needle in the north end of the gate.

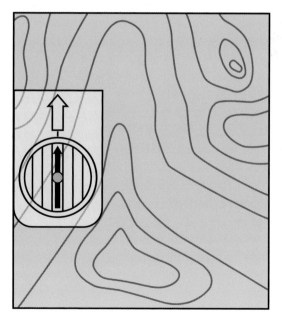

3-1 Orienting the map. For simplicity's sake the drawing assumes that true north and magnetic north lie in the same direction. All the remaining figures in this chapter use the same assumption.

And while you've got the map out, try to create a mental image of the terrain you'll be traveling through. Maybe you head east up that creek for 2 miles, then make a sharp left just past a big cliff, leaving the main trail and following a spur trail that climbs toward a pass to the north. Knowing that kind of thing will help you start looking for a trail junction at the appropriate time. Don't count on a sign to jolt you into looking up from your companion's boot heels.

Make it a habit during your hike to get out your map and compass every hour or so and locate your position on the map. Keep track of the time you started and the time it takes you to reach various landmarks—that trail junction, for example. It'll give you a sense of your pace that day, which will help you keep track of your location.

Identifying Landmarks Using Map and Compass

Let's say your goal for the day is the summit of some peak. You reach it at lunchtime and sit down to admire the enormous panorama of mountains spread out before you. Orienting your map will give you a rough idea which peak is which. If you want to know accurately, however, you'll need to get a bit more sophisticated.

First, take a bearing on the peak you're interested in, using the technique I described in the previous chapter. A glance back at figure 2-5 should refresh your memory. That bearing, you'll recall, is just the angle between a line heading north and a line leading to the peak. The angle is measured clockwise from the north line. Although you used the direction-of-travel arrow or notch in the mirror to sight the peak, note that you would have gotten exactly the same result if you'd sighted along one long edge of the baseplate.

Now you're going to transfer that angle to the map. One line of the angle, represented by the compass gate and the north-south lines inside the capsule, will point north; the other line, represented by one long edge of the baseplate, will run right through your position and toward the peak you're interested in.

To make the logic of the next step easier, orient the map before continuing and then reset the compass to the bearing you just measured. Now place the compass on the map so that the compass gate points north, toward the top of the map, and so that one long edge of the baseplate sits on top of your position. Note that the long edges of the gate (and the north-south lines in the capsule) run parallel to the right and left margins of the map. Don't twist the capsule in relation to the baseplate. Ignore the compass needle. You're simply using the compass as a protractor now, so the needle is irrelevant.

The long edge of the baseplate that is sitting atop your position now points directly at the peak you're interested in. Figure 3-2 shows a compass placed correctly

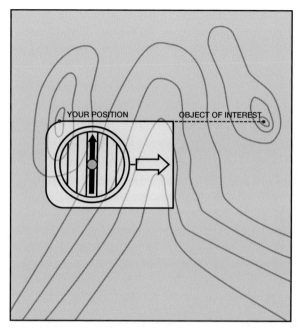

3-2 Applying a bearing taken in the field to the map. Make sure that one long edge of the compass sits on your position, that the north-south lines run north and south, and that the north end of the capsule points to the north end of the map.

on the map. Note—this is important—that you must make sure you follow the long edge of the baseplate in the direction indicated by the direction-of-travel arrow. With the map oriented correctly, you'll see that the long edge of the baseplate not only points to the paper mountain—it also points to the real one.

Technophiles among my readers should note that a GPS receiver can't easily tell you the name of that magnificent peak on the horizon. It can tell you where you are, but you already know that. The easiest way by far to identify landmarks when you know your position is a little old-fashioned map-and-compass work.

Measuring Courses on a Map

Your map and compass will also help you solve the opposite puzzle. Once again, let's assume you know where you are on the map. This time, though, you want to use the map to tell you which way to go. We faced this situation on the summit plateau of Mt. Hunter, for example. You'd face a similar problem if you were down in the woods at Lake Hereweare and wanted to know the direction to Lake Overthere.

To solve this problem, you need to measure an angle on the map and transfer it to the terrain. The angle, called a course, will be the angle between a line heading north and a line heading to your destination, with your position as the point (the vertex) of the angle.

Start by laying one of the long edges of the baseplate along an imaginary line connecting your position and your destination. Sometimes, as in figure 3-3, the baseplate will be long enough to extend between the two; at other times you'll need to mentally extrapolate a line along the long edge of the baseplate to position the baseplate accurately. (At home you can use a ruler to extend the line.) Be sure the direction-of-travel arrow points at your destination. Now twist the capsule until the gate points north, as shown in figure 3-4. Both the long edges of the gate and the north-south lines will run parallel to the left and right margins of the map. Once again, you're using the compass as a protractor, so the needle's gyrations are irrelevant. Read the course—the angle—at the index mark, where the direction-of-travel arrow abuts the compass dial.

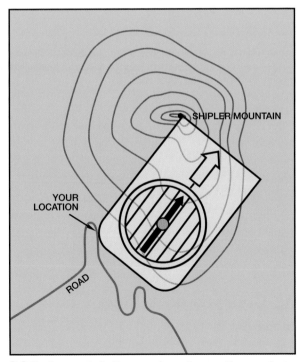

3-3 The first step in finding a course on the map. Place one long edge of the baseplate along an imaginary line connecting your position and your destination. Make sure the direction-of-travel arrow points at your destination.

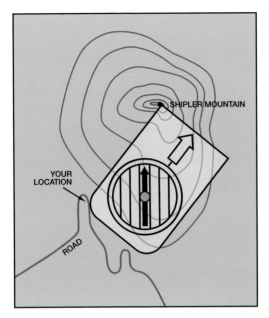

3-4 The second step in finding a course on the map. Rotate the capsule in relation to the baseplate until the north-south lines run north and south and the north end of the capsule points north.

To transfer that angle to the field, pick up your compass and rotate it as a unit, without moving the capsule in relation to the baseplate, until you've placed the needle in the gate. As shown in figure 3-5, the direction-of-travel arrow now points in the direction you want to go. Pick a nearby landmark, walk to it, pick another, and proceed.

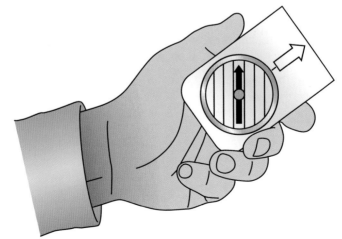

3-5 Using a course measured on a map to determine the direction to your destination in the field. Without rotating the capsule in relation to the baseplate, rotate the entire compass as a unit until the needle is aligned within the compass gate and the north end of the needle points to the north end of the capsule. The direction-of-travel arrow now points toward your destination.

If you're measuring a course at home as part of your trip-planning, you can use a ruler to align the north-south lines more accurately with true north and south. As before, place your compass so one long edge extends between your position and your destination. Butt your ruler up against that edge in such a way that one end of the ruler touches either the right or left edge of the map. Slide your compass along the ruler until the capsule is set over a margin. Now you can use the margin to align the north-south lines accurately. Figure 3-6 illustrates this technique.

The ruler won't always reach the edge of the map of course, and you need a flat surface to work on. But it's still a useful trick to know when you need high accuracy and conditions permit you to use it.

Now you're pointed in the right direction: You've got a course, taken from the map. But as three friends and I discovered during the first day of the Colorado Grand Tour, the game's not over. You haven't gotten there yet.

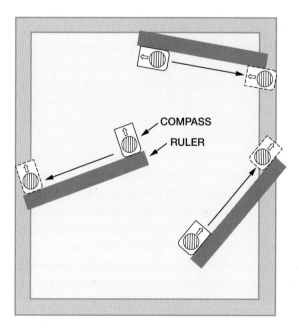

3-6 Using a ruler to align the north-south lines with the edges of the map.

Once again it was stormy, with intense winds and near-zero visibility. My friends were all ex–Outward Bound instructors; I had guided a couple of expeditions on Mt. McKinley. We were bound—we hoped—for Vail, 100 miles and seven days away. But the major storm blasting the Front Range was threatening to thwart us only hours after we started. We lunched at a drafty wilderness cabin and then climbed another quarter of a mile to a knoll clearly marked on the map. From there we needed to follow a broad ridge down through a saddle, then up to the snow-covered Rollins Pass Road. It didn't seem possible to get lost following a ridge. Furthermore, we'd all done this leg of the tour before. Just to be sure, Kim Miller dug out the map and compass and determined our course: 270 degrees straight west. We weren't going to commit the mistake Dale's search party made on James Peak. We pushed on, leaning into the wind like circus clowns with weighted shoes, our heads bowed, our faces so swaddled in face masks and goggles that we felt like astronauts walking on the moon.

A half hour slipped away—much longer than it should have taken to reach the steep climb leading up to the road. Kim pulled out his compass and called a halt.

"You guys," he said, "we're heading east." We crowded around in disbelief. In the storm we had walked in a complete semicircle and were facing the way we had come.

We righted our course and tried to hurry, but it was still two hours after dark when we arrived in Winter Park, our first night's stop. The moral was clear: When the weather is foul, you not only need to check your compass, you need to check it frequently. Correctly using it once doesn't guarantee safe arrival. Keep your compass in your pocket or hanging around your neck so you'll have no excuse not to use it.

Identifying Your Location from Known Landmarks

In the examples above, I assumed you knew your location on the map but wanted to know the name of a distant peak or the direction you should travel. Now let's assume you don't know your location, but you can identify some landmark, such as a prominent peak that you recognize.

Two friends and I encountered an easy example of that kind of problem on a Memorial Day hike to Ypsilon Lake in Rocky Mountain National Park. We knew basically where we were; we were on the trail to the lake. But the packs were heavy (we had overnight camping gear as well as ski-mountaineering equipment) and we wanted to know our exact location on the trail. (What we really wanted to know was how much longer we'd have to suffer beneath those packs.) So I took a bearing on the prominent shoulder of a nearby ridge. Once again I had an angle between a line running north and a line leading to a landmark. I knew that my position had to be along the line of the angle that passed through the ridge's shoulder. So I placed one long edge of the baseplate on the shoulder of the ridge and rotated the whole compass, without turning the capsule in relation to the baseplate, until the north-south lines ran north and south. The direction-of-travel arrow pointed at the landmark. Now I knew I had to be along the line defined by that long edge of the baseplate. I'll call that a line of position. Since I also knew I was on the trail, I had to be at the intersection of my line of position and the trail. Figure 3-7 shows this graphically.

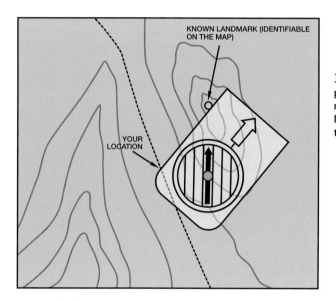

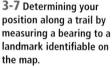

3-7 Determining your position along a trail by measuring a bearing to a landmark identifiable on the map.

If the edge of the baseplate hadn't reached from the shoulder to the trail, I would have estimated where the line of position crossed the trail. If I had really needed accuracy, I would have used a pencil to draw a line along the edge of the baseplate, then advanced the compass and extended the line of position until it crossed the trail.

You don't need to be on a trail to use this technique. You could just as well be following a stream, a river, a pronounced ridge, or the bank of a large lake. Any kind of prominent, linear terrain feature will do. In all cases the best accuracy comes from picking a landmark at right angles to the terrain feature you're following.

If you can identify two landmarks, you don't even need to be following a terrain feature. Simply take a bearing off one, and pencil in your line of position on the map. Then take a bearing off the second, and pencil in that line of position. Your location is the intersection of the two lines. Figure 3-8 shows you how. If

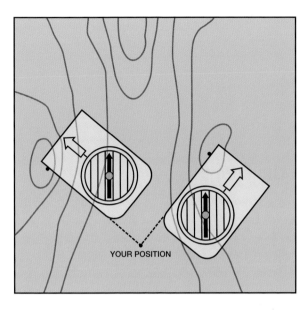

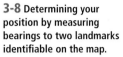 Determining your position by measuring bearings to two landmarks identifiable on the map.

you can take a bearing off a third landmark and pencil in that line of position, so much the better. In a perfect world the three lines would intersect at exactly the same place. In the real world the three lines probably won't intersect at a common point but rather form a triangle. Your true position should lie somewhere inside the triangle formed by the three lines of position.

Once you've identified your location with lines of position, perform a reality check. If the lines cross at a stream and you're standing on a ridge, something is wrong. After we identified our position along the trail to Ypsilon Lake, we took a close look at the map. We had just hiked up a steep section of trail and reached a nearly level stretch. Our line of position from the shoulder crossed the trail right where the contours suddenly became widely spaced—in other words, where the terrain abruptly flattened out. Our location as determined by a line of position agreed with the other information we had about the terrain. Whenever you use a map and compass together, it's a good idea to perform that kind of reality check on the results. The key to that is being able to visualize terrain from looking at a map. You can learn a certain amount of that from this book, but to really develop that skill, you need to practice out in the field.

Throughout this chapter I've employed a simplifying assumption: that true north and magnetic north lie in the same direction. Although that makes it easier to learn the principles of map-and-compass navigation, it's rarely true in the real world. In the next chapter I'll tell how to compensate for that difference.

How to Correct for Declination

Sometimes reading explanations of how to reconcile true north and magnetic north is like watching a clown cross his arms, point in opposite directions, and say, "He went thataway." But fear not: There are simple, easy-to-comprehend ways to solve declination problems. The best way, as I mentioned in Chapter 2, is to buy a set-and-forget compass. I'll show you how to use one later in this chapter, after I've laid the groundwork for you to understand the explanation.

Even if you didn't buy a set-and-forget compass, you can still learn to correct for declination. You don't need to memorize rules or silly rhymes; you just need to remember some straightforward logic.

Declination, as I've already mentioned, is the difference in direction between magnetic north and true north. Magnetic north is defined by the direction a compass needle points. True north, also called geographic north, is defined by the direction to the geographic North Pole—one end of the Earth's axis of rotation. Declination, therefore, is an angle. It's measured with true north as the starting point. If magnetic north lies to the east of true north (to the right, or clockwise, as we look at a map), we say the declination is east. If magnetic north lies to the west of true north (to the left, or counterclockwise), we say the declination is west. East declination is measured clockwise from true north; west declination is measured counterclockwise. (This is in contrast to bearings and courses, which are always measured clockwise.) In other words, if magnetic north lies 10 degrees east of true north, the declination is 10 degrees east. If magnetic north lies 10 degrees west of true north, the declination is 10 degrees west, not 350 degrees.

Declination in the United States varies from about 20 degrees west in Maine to 21 degrees east in Washington and as much as 30 degrees east in parts of Alaska. The *agonic line,* where the declination is zero, runs from the Great Lakes to Florida. Ignoring the correction for declination can lead you seriously astray and raise the rude possibility of eating shoe leather for dinner as you bask in the warmth of your cigarette lighter. For each degree that your course is in error and each mile that you travel, you'll be off by 92 feet. If the declination is 20 degrees, you'll be off by 1,834 feet—one-third of a mile—after hiking just 1 mile. It's pretty hard to relocate your tent if a third of a mile of timber or fog separates you from it.

Strictly speaking, it's incorrect to say, "The compass needle points to the magnetic north pole." What the needle actually does is align itself with the Earth's magnetic field. That magnetic field resembles a skein of yarn when the cat's done playing with it. Compass needles may or may not actually point at the magnetic north pole itself, which in 2007 was near Canada's Ellesmere Island and moving toward Russia at a rate of around 35 miles per year. For the sake of simplicity, let's just say the compass needle points to magnetic north.

For a wilderness traveler the exact position of the magnetic north pole doesn't matter. If you're using the most recent USGS map available, the declination it gives will be accurate within a degree or two. If you need the most up-to-date value for the declination, visit www.ngdc.noaa.gov/geomagmodels/IGRF.jsp, a website run by the National Geophysical Data Center, a division of the National Oceanic and Atmospheric Administration. There you can search for the current declination by entering the latitude and longitude of the region where you'll be traveling, or search by zip code. Handheld compasses, even mirror-sight ones, are only accurate plus or minus about 2 degrees, so such precision is unnecessary unless you are using a tripod-mounted pocket transit, which is essentially a highly accurate compass and inclinometer. I actually purchased a Brunton Pocket Transit when I was working on a series of photographs in Arches National Park where I needed extreme precision (plus or minus half a degree) in calculating the position of the sun and moon, but I've never needed my pocket transit for navigation.

Although declination changes slowly as you travel east or west, you can assume that the needle always points in the same direction within the bounds of the area you can cover in a typical human-powered trip. On the East Coast, for example, where declination changes relatively quickly, you'd have to travel east or west at least 50 miles for the declination to change 1 degree.

All USGS maps have a declination diagram in the bottom margin similar to the one shown in figure 4-1, which happens to show a declination of 14 degrees west. True north is always indicated by the line with a star, which symbolizes Polaris, the North Star. The magnetic north line is indicated by "MN." On some maps, grid north, a concept we don't need to worry about, is indicated "GN." The amount of declination, in degrees, is written beside the diagram.

Correcting for Declination with a Standard Compass

Let's assume for the moment that you didn't spend the extra money to buy a set-and-forget compass. (If you did, consider your money well spent and skip ahead to the section below labeled "Using a Set-and-Forget Compass.") Before you can understand how to correct for declination with a standard baseplate compass, you need to ingrain two facts in your mind. First, every angle that you measure on a *map* is measured clockwise, with *true north* as the starting point. The needle is irrelevant. You're simply using the compass as a protractor. Second, every angle that you measure in the *field* by placing the needle in the gate of the compass is also measured clockwise, but the starting point is *magnetic north.*

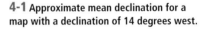

MN   14°   ★

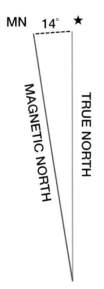

MAGNETIC NORTH

TRUE NORTH

4-1 Approximate mean declination for a map with a declination of 14 degrees west.

Let's refer to angles with true north as the starting point as true north bearings or true north courses. (They're essentially the same. A bearing is just a direction to a landmark; a course is a direction you'll follow.) All angles measured on a map, starting from true north, will be true north bearings or true north courses. All angles measured with a standard compass, using magnetic north as the starting point, will be magnetic north bearings or magnetic north courses.

Now let's assume that you're hiking in the Colorado Rockies, where the declination is always east. Take a look at figure 4-2. True north is marked zero degrees. Magnetic north is marked 10 degrees. It lies to the east of true north.

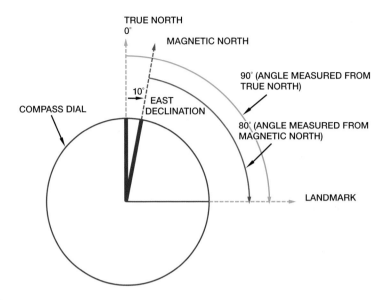

4-2 The relationship between true north angles and magnetic north angles for a declination of 10 degrees east.

In other words, the declination is 10 degrees east. Now let's say you measure a course on the map to a landmark and find it to be 90 degrees. That's a true north course; you started measuring at true north, just as the diagram shows. Now if you take a bearing on that same landmark with your compass, you'll find the bearing to be 80 degrees. That's a magnetic north bearing, since you started measuring at magnetic north.

The true north angle, measured on the map, is greater than the magnetic north angle, measured in the field with the compass by placing the needle in the gate. Furthermore, the difference is 10 degrees—exactly the amount of the declination. And that leads to our first conclusion: *When the declination is east, true north angles (bearings and courses) are always going to be greater than magnetic north angles (bearings and courses).* If you measure an angle on the map and want to transfer it to your compass, you must *subtract* the declination from the true north angle, because magnetic north angles are always smaller than true north angles when the declination is east. If you measure an angle with your compass and want to transfer it to the map, you must *add* the declination, because true north angles are always greater than magnetic north angles when the declination is east.

You don't need to memorize these rules. Just remember the logic behind them. If you need to jog your memory, look at the declination diagram on the bottom of the map. Notice how it closely resembles the part of figure 4-2 that is drawn with heavy lines. If magnetic north is east (clockwise, or to the right) of true north, then every angle measured clockwise from true north must be greater than the same angle measured clockwise from magnetic north. To reinforce this concept one more time, look at figure 4-3. It shows the relationship between magnetic north and true north for a situation where the true north bearing is 270 degrees.

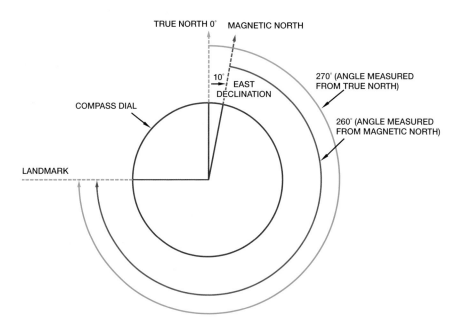

4-3 A second example of the relationship between true north angles and magnetic north angles for a declination of 10 degrees east.

The same logic applies if the declination is west, as it is on the East Coast. Look at figure 4-4. The declination is again 10 degrees, but this time it's west. Let's say you measure an angle on the map (starting at true north) as 90 degrees. If you measure the same angle in the field with your compass, starting at magnetic north, you'll get 100 degrees. The difference, 10 degrees, is equal to the declination. That leads to our second conclusion: When the declination is west, true north angles (bearings and courses) are always going to be smaller than magnetic north angles (bearings and courses).

If you measure an angle on the map and want to transfer it to your compass, you must *add* the declination to the true north angle, because magnetic north angles are always greater than true north angles when the declination is west. If you measure an angle with your compass and want to transfer it to the map, you must *subtract* the declination from the magnetic angle for the same reason: True north angles are always smaller than magnetic north angles when the declination is west. Again, the declination diagram in the bottom margin of the map should help refresh your memory should you ever forget.

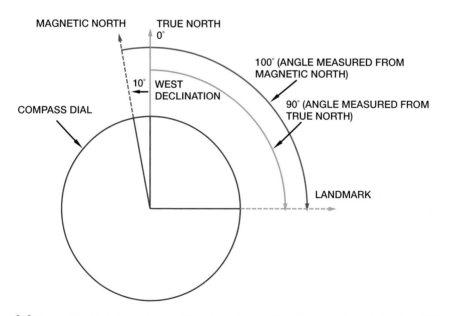

4-4 The relationship between true north angles and magnetic north angles for a declination of 10 degrees west.

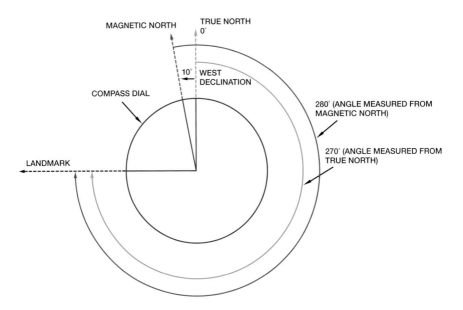

4-5 A second example of the relationship between true north angles and magnetic north angles for a declination of 10 degrees west.

Figure 4-5 gives another example of the relation between magnetic and true north when the declination is west, this time for a true north angle of 270 degrees.

Sometimes in the East you'll measure a true north angle on the map and then find when you add the west declination that you've gone past 360 degrees. For example, you might measure a true north angle on the map as 355 degrees, then need to add a declination of 10 degrees west to get the magnetic angle: 355 + 10 = 365. An angle of 365 degrees is the same as an angle of 5 degrees. You can also just rotate the compass dial counterclockwise 10 degrees to add 10 degrees to the true north angle of 355 degrees and get the correct magnetic north angle of 5 degrees. Figure 4-6 shows this graphically.

Sometimes in the West you'll measure a true north angle on the map, find it's less than the declination, then need to subtract the declination from the true north angle to get the magnetic north angle. For example, the true north angle, measured on the map, might be 5 degrees, and you'll have to subtract a declination of 10 degrees east. Five degrees is the same as 365 degrees, so you can just subtract 10 from 365 and get 355 degrees as the correct magnetic north angle. You can also just rotate the dial clockwise 10 degrees from its original setting of 5 degrees to do the subtraction and reach the correct magnetic north setting of 355 degrees. Figure 4-7 shows this graphically.

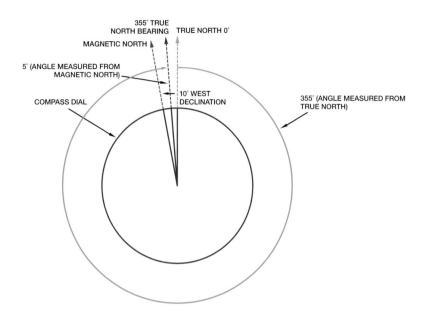

4-6 The relationship between a true north angle of 355 degrees and a magnetic north angle of 5 degrees when the declination is 10 degrees west.

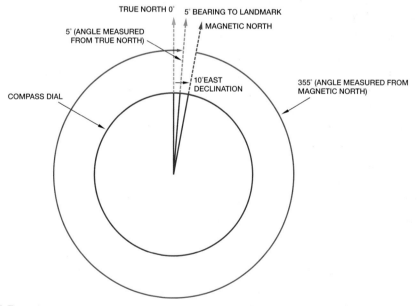

4-7 The relationship between a true north angle of 5 degrees and a magnetic north angle of 355 degrees when the declination is 10 degrees east.

Using a Set-and-Forget Compass

If you're using a set-and-forget compass, draw a big sigh of relief at this point. You can forget about adding and subtracting angles once you've set the declination and double-checked that you set it in the right direction. With most such compasses setting the declination is idiot-proof. Usually you turn a small screw or perform some other simple operation to adjust the compass gate so it points to the angle representing the declination. If the declination is 20 degrees east, for example, the compass gate, after adjustment, will point to 20 degrees. If the declination is 20 degrees west, the compass gate, after adjustment, will point to 340 degrees (360 − 20 = 340). When you're measuring an angle on the map with a set-and-forget compass, you ignore the needle (as always) and the compass gate (which no longer points to north on the capsule). Instead you always use the capsule's north-south lines when you're orienting the capsule north and south, making sure north on the capsule points to north on the map. To transfer that angle to your compass, simply place the needle in the gate. Angles measured with your compass can be transferred directly to the map, again using the north-south lines in the capsule, not the gate. As you can see, set-and-forget compasses let you avoid mental gymnastics when you're cold and wet and would much rather be thinking about dinner courses than compass courses. If you plan to go hiking more than once this year, buy a set-and-forget compass. You'll never regret it.

When Theory Meets the Real World

When we awoke at our camp on the Kahiltna Glacier, menacing clouds had already encircled Mt. McKinley's 20,320-foot summit, 2 vertical miles above us. By midmorning, when we started hauling a sled-load of supplies up the glacier, the cloud ceiling had plunged to 10,000 feet and snow was falling so thickly we inhaled dozens of huge flakes at every breath.

In May, the peak climbing season, the Kahiltna Glacier is so heavily traveled by climbers attempting the West Buttress route that a virtual trail leads to the summit. Skis, snowshoes, and boots pack a trench into the snow as climbers avoid trail-breaking by following in each other's footsteps. Climbers further mark the trail with bamboo wands flagged with orange surveyor's tape. Heavy storms, however, like the one now assaulting the mountain, knock down and bury the wands and fill in the trail. Landmarks vanish, and a whiteout ensues. Glacier, clouds, and mountain become indistinguishable, and all sense of direction vanishes. I've seen climbers in whiteouts step calmly off 5-foot-high ice cliffs, completely oblivious to the cliff's existence until they planted a foot firmly in air.

Such a whiteout was quickly overtaking us. We had anticipated that the West Buttress would be crawling with the usual hordes of climbers, their packs sporting orange forests of wands, and so we had brought only a few wands of our own. Now we were regretting that decision. Only a few wands marked the trail behind us, and drifting snow was rapidly filling the track itself. Soon all trace of the route back to our tents would disappear. The tents themselves would be invisible from only 50 yards away. Continuing uphill now might make relocating our camp a few hours later difficult indeed.

I called a halt and urged my teammates to retreat for the day. Reluctantly they agreed. We cached our loads and bolted for camp.

Fortunately several teams behind us had beaten down the trail, so finding our tents turned out to be easy. My friends gave me glances that said, "Next time, don't be such a wimp." We settled into our sleeping bags to wait for better weather.

In the morning, when I slipped out of the tent, I saw a line of climbers appearing slowly, one by one, over a low ice hummock well off the correct route. Each step seemed to demand tremendous effort. Their haggard faces told of a sleepless night. Soon their story unfolded. All were from the University of Idaho. They had pushed a little higher than we had the day before, turned back a little later. The trail had vanished, buried by wind-driven fresh snow. When they reached the level glacier only a quarter of a mile from their tents, they lost their way completely. Tired, in failing light, they dug a huge snow cave and waited for dawn, without sleeping bags, foam pads, food, or water. The temperature dropped to 15 degrees.

This incident occurred in 1987, long before GPS units were readily available. It's a textbook example of a situation where a GPS receiver would have been invaluable. Today I wouldn't embark on a major mountaineering expedition without one.

Even in 1987, however, foresight could have prevented a very unpleasant night. On glaciers and big snowfields, where whiteouts can sweep in quickly, it's often essential to create your own landmarks by placing wands every 180 feet or so. Climbers should always travel roped up on a big glacier as protection against falling into a crevasse. Most teams use a 150-foot rope. If the wands are spaced every 180 feet, the second climber can stay at a wand while the leader goes out to find the next. That way the team is never out of sight of a wand.

Once the Idaho climbers lost the trail, they had few options. Bivouacking in a snow cave, out of the wind, where they could share body heat, probably prevented any serious hypothermia. If they had been determined to keep searching, their best bet would probably have been to head back uphill, using a course taken off the map, until they reached the first steep rise—proof positive that they were above their tents. Then they could have zigzagged slowly up the slope, from one side of the glacier to the other, until they found one of the remaining wands. From there they could have measured a course on the map straight down the glacier. Then, after fanning out but remaining in sight of each other, they could have started searching, following the bearing downhill. The method certainly wouldn't guarantee them finding their tents, but it would at least keep them moving and warm until morning.

Another glacier 8,500 miles away in Argentina put me in a predicament similar to the Idahoans'. The experience taught me a lot about navigating in the real world.

I was making a one-day, solo attempt on the summit of Aconcagua, the highest mountain in the Western Hemisphere at 22,834 feet. I had started at 19,000 feet, at the foot of the Polish Glacier, at 2 a.m. Thirteen hours later I was still 500 feet below the summit. A flu virus had stolen my voice, my muscles had become lard, and a flotilla of black clouds was rolling in from the Pacific. I headed down.

And none too soon. By the time I reached the broad snow bowl at the foot of the glacier, it was nearly dark. A few wands materialized out of the gloom, left by some previous expedition. They seemed to be leading too far to the right, or south, but I followed them anyway. I knew that just beyond the foot of the glacier was the top of a large cliff. My camp lay below the cliff; I had walked around the north end of the cliff in the predawn darkness sixteen hours before. The clifftop would act as a *catching feature,* alerting me that I needed to turn left, to the north, to begin my end run around the cliff.

I walked off snow onto rock and stumbled ahead. Suddenly an abyss yawned before me out of the darkness and flying snow. I had reached the clifftop. The crux now was to find my way back through the complex, broken cliff bands that formed the north end of the cliff.

I began scrambling northward along the junction of snow and rock, thinking I was only minutes from my tent. But nothing looked familiar. The cliff shrank and ended, but now I confronted a talus field studded with outcrops and small cliff bands. In darkness and storm, dehydrated and exhausted, I could not find the way back to my tent. I croaked, "Hello, anybody there?" a couple of times but got no reply. I started thinking about digging a snow cave and waiting for dawn.

Then, barely audible over the wind, I heard a voice. I stumbled in that direction. A tent appeared, inhabited by some American climbers. They pointed me in the right direction at last, and I soon found my tent only 300 yards away. Too exhausted to eat the dinner my body desperately needed, I drank a quart of soup and collapsed into my bag.

I had made a serious mistake that had almost cost me a forced bivouac on a subzero night at 19,000 feet. I hadn't built a cairn, or series of cairns, to guide me around the cliff. After all, the weather had been perfectly clear when I started, and I expected to be back before dark—the oft-repeated refrain of lost hikers and climbers everywhere. In situations like that, it's best to plan for the worst case, not the best.

How "Aiming Off" Can Help You Find Your Way

But I had done some things right. I had used a technique called "aiming off." Instead of aiming directly for the north end of the cliff, I had aimed to the right. Then, when I reached the edge of the glacier, I knew I had to turn left. If I had aimed directly for the cliff end and missed even slightly, I would have wasted even more time than I did wandering in the dark amidst the cliff bands and outcrops forming the cliff's indistinct end, wondering whether to go right or left.

You can apply the same technique to following a course through the woods back to a road where you parked your car. It's impossible to follow a course with complete accuracy. If you miss by even a couple hundred yards, your car may be hidden by a bend in the road and you won't know which way to turn. So instead of aiming directly for the car, set your course about 10 degrees off. Then, when you hit the road, you know which way to turn.

The same principle applies in other situations: finding a bridge or ford across a creek, a snow bridge across a lengthy crevasse, a camp you've placed along the shore of a large lake. Road, creek, crevasse, and lakeshore are all "catching features": They tell you unmistakably that it's time to change course. Once you've made the turn, they can be considered *handrails*. You can follow them without further references to your map or compass. Thinking about those two concepts can often make your route-finding easier. Instead of heading cross-country for several miles, navigating through thick woods with a compass, it may well be easier to walk an extra quarter mile to a stream or lakeshore that parallels your course and serves as a handrail. It will almost certainly be easier to walk that far to a trail rather than bushwhack. Then look for a catching feature to tell you when to resume your original course. It might be a prominent side stream. It could also be a particular bearing on a prominent peak that you can see from the handrail.

It's all too easy, when you're traveling through the woods, to decide you've reached the feature you want to use as your handrail when you actually haven't. In fact, it's remarkably easy, if you're careless or in a hurry, to make the map seem to fit what you're looking at in any situation. Joe Kaelin and I demonstrated that perfectly in 1979 in the Canadian Rockies.

Admittedly the map was poor: a 1:250,000-scale topo on which 1 inch equaled 4 miles. And the clouds were hanging only a few hundred feet above the valley floor. Our intent was to cross the Sunwapta River and hike up Habel Creek to Wooley Shoulder. We made a crude estimate of the distance we should drive from Sunwapta Pass to reach the junction of Habel Creek and the Sunwapta River. When we'd driven about that far, we spotted a side creek and told the driver who had given us a lift to drop us off.

After three hours of hard work and 2,000 feet of elevation gain, the fog lifted from both the terrain and our minds. We realized we were in entirely the wrong drainage. Habel Creek intersected the Sunwapta a mile farther downriver. We descended almost 2,000 feet, reached the right creek, and climbed 3,000 feet to Wooley Shoulder.

Even with our small-scale map, we should have done much better. Habel Creek clearly occupied a deep valley much larger and much less precipitous than the one we'd so laboriously climbed. Any kind of careful map study would have told us very quickly that we were gaining elevation much too fast and were in much too shallow a ravine to be in the Habel Creek valley. More careful measurement of the distance from Sunwapta Pass to our drop-off point would also have helped us get started correctly.

A couple of years later, when I was a bit wiser, I encountered a similar situation on my trip to Aconcagua. Our map there had 500-*meter* contour intervals. Once again we were traveling along a major river, the Rio de las Vacas, and were looking for a side canyon occupied by a stream called the Relincho. The Relincho, we knew, drained the entire eastern side of Aconcagua, including the Polish Glacier. We passed several side canyons, including one the assistant guide thought for sure contained the Relincho. But none of the side canyons seemed to me big enough to contain the outflow of a major glacier. A few miles farther up the Vacas, we turned a corner and found ourselves gazing up a deep side valley at Aconcagua rising 2 vertical miles above us.

As my experience on Aconcagua and in Canada shows, simply identifying valleys and side canyons on the map, without considering scale, is not enough. You have to use your head too.

What to Do if You Think You're Lost

Using your head is good advice as well for correcting route-finding mistakes that have left you temporarily confused, shall we say, about your location. If you've been identifying your position on the map periodically and kept track of the direction you've been traveling, you can't really become lost. All you need to do is backtrack to your last known location and then think through all the possible errors you could have made after you first passed that location. Since there's always a possibility that you will need to reverse course, for many reasons besides getting lost, you should glance over your shoulder frequently to memorize what your route looks like when you're heading in the opposite direction.

If you've been following a course and think you should have reached your destination by now but haven't, stop and analyze possible mistakes. Did you compensate for declination? Did you compensate in the right direction? Could you have overshot your destination? Or are you just moving more slowly than you thought, and it's still ahead? Often it pays to go to a nearby clearing or bare-topped knoll. The clear view may help you identify landmarks. Whatever you do, don't panic, and don't blunder off in some hastily chosen direction, compounding your confusion.

Following a stream downhill is *sometimes* good advice, if you're in a pretty civilized area well cut by roads. In real wilderness, however, you could find yourself walking a long, long way. In Canyonlands National Park, for example, following a stream downhill could take you to the Colorado River. No road parallels the river; there isn't even a bridge *across* the river for a hundred miles.

If you're absolutely convinced you cannot determine your location, and if you notified someone where you were going and when you expected to be back, your best bet is to stay put and wait for searchers to find you. Nearly all wild areas in this country are within the response area of some kind of search-and-rescue organization. You'll make their job easier if you can move to a nearby location that's easily visible from the air and the surrounding terrain—a ridgetop or some kind of clearing. Building a small fire—*if* you're *utterly* convinced you can keep it under control—makes you easier to spot and will certainly keep you warmer inside and out.

But all this doom-and-gloom stuff should happen to the other guy, not to you, if you find your position on the map at the beginning of your trip, pinpoint your position periodically, and always know the direction you're traveling. Sure, a GPS receiver is a great backup if you truly get lost, but that's a subject for another chapter.

Altimeter Navigation

It was 2:50 a.m. and I'd already been grinding up the trail leading to the summit of 14,309-foot Uncompahgre Peak for an hour. My goal was to shoot sunrise from the summit, so I had a deadline. Sunrise waits for no photographer.

I glanced at the altimeter strapped to my wrist and suddenly became worried. I was pushing hard, yet the altimeter showed that I had gained only 770 feet since leaving the trailhead exactly one hour earlier. I knew my pace would slump as I reached higher altitudes. A quick mental calculation showed that I was moving too slowly. I had 2,900 feet to gain from the trailhead and less than four hours to do it. At the rate I was going, I could easily miss sunrise. This was the third day in a row in which I had gotten up at 1 a.m. to climb a 14,000-foot peak in the dark. Clearly I had not fully recovered from the first two efforts.

I increased my pace still further, testing the limits of my aerobic capacity. Feeling rather sick, with only minutes to spare, I finally arrived on the summit. Hastily I set up my 4×5 large-format field camera and had the great good fortune to capture spectacular sunrise light on the graceful cirrus clouds above Wetterhorn Peak.

On steep trails like that on Uncompahgre Peak, elevation gained per hour is often a better gauge of your pace than miles traveled per hour. Even an old-fashioned mechanical altimeter lets you calculate your pace by subtracting your starting elevation from your current elevation every hour. Modern electronic altimeters do the arithmetic for you by offering an altitude-difference mode that tells you the elevation gain and time elapsed since you last zeroed the altitude-difference setting. If you know your pace, of course, you can estimate your time of arrival more accurately.

For example, if you know from the map that the lake is at 9,000 feet and the pass is at 12,000 feet, you can take note of the time when you leave the lake and estimate your rate of ascent and time of arrival by how long it takes to climb the first 500 or 1,000 feet. If you leave the lake at 8 a.m. and take an hour to climb the first 1,000 feet, you can estimate you'll take three hours to climb 3,000 feet, which will put you at the pass at 11 a.m. In reality, with rest stops and fatigue, you'll probably arrive a little later.

Most electronic altimeters look like overgrown watches and in fact have all the normal watch functions. They're much lighter and less bulky than the typical handheld GPS unit. Some manufacturers of handheld GPS receivers have recognized the value of an altimeter and begun including one in some higher-end models. If you're planning to bring a GPS receiver regardless, these devices let you combine two tools into one.

Altimeters are also highly useful navigational tools. In the dark or in a whiteout, with no landmarks visible and no possibility of taking a compass bearing, an altimeter can sometimes pinpoint your location much faster than a GPS receiver. One glance at the altimeter gives you the elevation of the contour line you're on. If you have a second line of position—you know you're on a particular trail, for example, or following a particular stream or ridge crest—then your position is pinpointed exactly. You're standing at the intersection of the contour line and the second line of position.

Sometimes, particularly if you're following a trail or ridge, your contour line will intersect twice. In that case, having even the vaguest idea of where you are (which side of the pass you're on, for example) should tell you your location exactly.

Figure 6-1 shows two examples. If your altimeter reads 10,000 feet and you know you're on the trail to Chasm Lake, then you know you're at point A, where

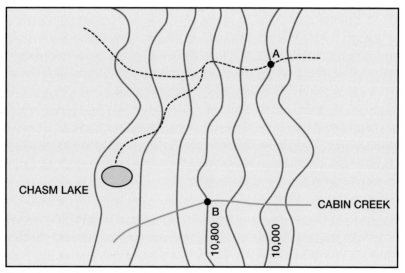

6-1 Using an altimeter and another line of position (such as a trail or creek) to determine your position.

the 10,000-foot contour line intersects the trail. Since that contour line intersects the trail only once, there can be no confusion. If it intersected twice, you would have to determine which of the two intersections marked your position by other means: the general lay of the land, the time spent on the trail, and your estimate of your pace.

In the second example, let's say you're bushwhacking up Cabin Creek and your altimeter reads 10,800 feet. You know you're at point B, where the creek intersects that contour. The same contour line never intersects a stream twice, of course, because streams constantly flow downhill.

The second line of position can also be a compass bearing. Perhaps you're in thick woods and get a glimpse of an identifiable peak. Or perhaps you're above timberline in a storm and get a glimpse through a hole in the clouds of some identifiable pass. With a little luck the compass bearing will cross the contour line indicated by your altimeter at something close to a right angle. If, however, the bearing runs parallel to your contour line, all you've done is confirm your altimeter's reading. You can't pinpoint your position, although you might be able to narrow it down, depending on the exact shape of the contour line. Mountaineers often find altimeters valuable even when a compass is useless and a map serves only to indicate the elevation of the top and bottom of the climb. On a first ascent on the north face of Alaska's Mt. Foraker in 1983, we used an altimeter to keep track of our progress up a steep rib. Since we were making very little horizontal distance on the map, compass bearings couldn't pinpoint our position. Our altimeter, though, let us gauge our rate of ascent and ration our food accordingly.

In some situations your compass, altimeter, and map can pinpoint your location even in a whiteout. The key to this direction-of-slope method is using the compass to determine the bearing of an imaginary line pointing straight downhill. Skiers would call it the fall line. By definition, that line will be perpendicular to the contour line (determined by your altimeter) on which your position lies. Take a look at figure 6-2. If your altimeter tells you you're on the 10,200-foot contour, for example, and your direction-of-slope line runs at a bearing of 150 degrees—southeast—you know you must be at position A. If the bearing is 210 degrees, you know your location must be position B.

This method won't help you everywhere, obviously. You can't determine your position on a broad hillside resembling a tilted tabletop, for example, nor can it help you if the hillside is cut by multiple ravines and you don't know which ridge or ravine you're in. But knowledge of this method would have helped prevent three friends and me from getting lost on the Commando Run, a ski tour from Vail Pass to Vail, Colorado. The dotted line on figure 6-2 shows the route we

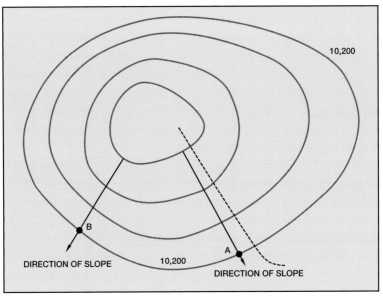

6-2 Using an altimeter and the direction-of-slope method to determine your position. The dotted line shows the route we should have taken. We actually started climbing the hillside at point B, where the slope was significantly steeper.

should have taken. Instead of climbing the hill there, however, where the slope was gentle, we continued contouring at the 10,200-foot level until we reached point B. When we finally turned uphill, we found ourselves forced to switchback repeatedly, an exhausting and tedious process, and then cross a steep and avalanche-prone chute at the very top of the slope. A quick map check an hour earlier would have saved a lot of energy.

Choosing an Altimeter

In all of the techniques I've just described, the accuracy of your position estimate depends on the accuracy of your altimeter. Accuracy depends in part, of course, on how much you spend, but it also depends, to a large degree, on you. To maximize your altimeter's usefulness and minimize possible errors, you need to know a little bit about how altimeters work.

Altimeters are closely related to barometers. Both work by measuring air pressure: in effect, the weight of a column of air rising above the instrument's position. The higher you go, the less atmosphere lies above you. Altimeters translate the air pressure at your location into an altitude reading.

Both mechanical altimeters and electronic ones use a small, sealed metal capsule to sense air pressure. Most of the air inside is removed during manufacturing, so a partial vacuum exists. As the pressure outside the capsule varies, the walls of the capsule flex in and out. In a mechanical altimeter those movements, which are only a few thousandths of an inch, are translated via a complex mechanism to the movements of a pointer, which rotates around a dial to indicate the elevation. In an electronic altimeter a special wire crisscrosses the surface of the capsule, forming what's called a "strain gauge." As the surface of the capsule flexes in and out with changing pressure, the wire is stretched slightly or allowed to relax. That changes its electrical resistance. Complex circuits translate that change in resistance into a voltage, which in turn is converted into a pressure reading.

All metals expand and contract as the temperature fluctuates. Really cheap altimeters can't compensate for that, which means that a change in their temperature causes them to register an apparent change in altitude even when the instrument is stationary and the pressure unvarying. Using a cheap altimeter that's not temperature-compensated can lead to errors of as much as 600 feet if you take the instrument out of a warm pocket and let it chill to ambient temperature on a wintry day. To minimize such errors, let the altimeter adjust to the prevailing temperature before setting it to your starting altitude. Then keep the altimeter in an outside pocket of your pack so it remains at approximately the same temperature.

Better instruments incorporate some element in their design that counteracts the effect of changing temperature. Mechanical altimeters usually use a bimetallic strip made of two metals fused together that have widely different rates of expansion and contraction when heated or cooled. When the strip is heated, for example, the strip bends away from the metal that expands the fastest. That bending is used to counteract expansion in other parts of the instrument that would otherwise lead to an apparent change in altitude.

Electronic altimeters also require temperature compensation, since the resistance of the strain gauge changes with temperature. Most use a second sensing element (another strain gauge, in other words) that is not bonded to the surface of the capsule and so is not under strain. This second sensing element is wired so its output cancels out changes in output from the primary sensor that are due solely to temperature changes. You can control one potential source of error, therefore, simply by buying a high-quality, temperature-compensated instrument.

Maintaining Your Altimeter's Accuracy

There are two other sources of error, however, that *you* must control. The first type of error arises because air pressure fluctuates constantly, even at the same elevation, as the weather changes. Changes in pressure cause the elevation reading to change. If you're moving up or down in elevation at the same time, it's impossible for you to sort out the two influences, and your altimeter can't tell the difference.

The only solution is to reset your altimeter, as often as possible, at known elevation points—the trailhead (always!), a pass, a lake, a summit, or the point where a trail crosses a stream or cuts across a prominent ridge. If you arrive at a lake that the map tells you is at 3,000 feet, for example, and your altimeter tells you it's at 3,100 feet, you can adjust the altimeter back down to 3,000 feet. If you can reset your altimeter every hour or so, you can limit the error due to weather to 40 feet or less. With a mechanical altimeter resetting the "reference altitude," as it is called, is a matter of turning a large dial in relation to the pointer. With an electronic altimeter it's usually a matter of entering the altitude mode, then resetting the altitude as you might reset the time on a watch.

Larger errors due to weather are common when you camp somewhere for a day or longer. If there is a major weather change during the night, for example, the difference between evening and morning readings can easily be several hundred feet. If you know the exact elevation of your camp from the map, you can correct as you normally would. If you can't determine your elevation from the map, the best way to maintain the accuracy of your altimeter readings is to note the reading when you arrive in camp and then reset the altimeter to that reading when you leave.

A second source of error is more subtle. All altimeters need some standardized method to convert pressure into altitude. They do this by referring to an internal database of standard pressures at different altitudes called the US Standard Atmosphere. That database must include a standard temperature as well, however, because cold air is denser and therefore heavier than warm air. A problem arises, therefore, if the temperature of the air through which you're traveling is different from the standard temperature for your elevation. If the air is warmer than the temperature used in the standard-atmosphere database, your altimeter will underestimate the actual elevation change. The air is less dense, and therefore a 1,000-foot change in actual elevation will not be accompanied by as big a change in pressure as predicted by the standard atmosphere. Your altimeter therefore reads low when you're climbing and high when you're descending. To give you a concrete example, if you hike on a warm summer day from the trailhead at 9,000 feet to a pass at 12,250 feet, your altimeter might read only 12,000 feet at your destination—an error of 250 feet. If you reset your altimeter to the correct elevation of 12,250 feet before beginning your descent, it will be reading high by about 250 feet when you reach the trailhead.

In a similar way, on a very cold winter day your altimeter will overestimate the altitude change as you gain or lose elevation. Going up, it will read high; going down, it will read low.

Standard-atmosphere temperatures are calculated by averaging the day and night temperature year-round, so they're usually colder than you actually experience in summer during the day, when most people go hiking. For example, the standard-atmosphere chart shows a temperature of 32 degrees for an elevation of 7,500 feet. As anyone who has visited the Rockies in summer knows, temperatures at that elevation during the day are nowhere near that cold. In Estes Park, for example, at 7,500 feet, the average high in July is 78 degrees.

You can correct for this elevation error if you have a thermometer, a calculator, and a standard-atmosphere chart with you, but it's not worth the bother. The easiest way to correct both for errors due to weather changes and errors as you move up and down in an atmosphere that is not at the standard reference temperature is simply to reset the altimeter at known elevation points as frequently as possible. With less effort than it takes to sight a single landmark and plot the bearing on the map, your altimeter will then serve you well as a navigational tool.

How the Global Positioning System Has Revolutionized Backcountry Navigation

For the last five years, I've been working on a series of photographs shot at sunrise from the summits of Colorado's 14,000-foot peaks. My goal has been to capture the exhilarating, humbling, and awe-inspiring experience of being a tiny speck on top of the world. For reasons I detailed in the introduction, the only safe way to be on the summit of a Fourteener at sunrise is to climb the peak in the dark. That, in turn, has posed the greatest backcountry navigation and route-finding challenges of my career—challenges where a GPS receiver, in combination with a map, compass, and altimeter, has sometimes been invaluable.

Here's an example. The Needle Mountains, a part of Colorado's San Juan Mountains, are justifiably famous among mountaineers. Even today they require a full day to approach them. When Franklin Rhoda, a member of the 1874 Hayden Survey, saw the Needle Mountains in the distance from the summit of Mt. Sneffels, he wrote, "We have never yet seen the group from any station (and we have viewed it from all sides) without feeling both deep respect and awe for their terrible ruggedness."

In July 2006 I rode the Durango and Silverton Narrow-Gauge Railroad to Needleton and then backpacked 6 miles in to Chicago Basin, base camp for the Needle Mountains' three Fourteeners: Sunlight, Windom, and Eolus. The next morning my alarm jarred me awake at 1 a.m. Map study had convinced me that Sunlight Peak probably offered the best composition, so I started with it. My plan had one hitch: I'd never climbed any of these peaks, and trying to find my way up routes requiring difficult scrambling—in the dark, by headlamp, with about forty pounds of 4 × 5 camera gear on my back—was a daunting challenge. Still, nothing ventured, nothing gained. The worst that could happen, I thought, was that I'd sit down on some ledge in the dark, put on all my warm clothes, and wait for the sun to come up so I could find my way back down.

A steep but straightforward trail led to Twin Lakes and then into the basin below Sunlight and Windom Peaks. From there things got trickier. I knew I was supposed to climb a gully called the Red Couloir. In the dark, of course, all colors are indistinguishable, even with the aid of moonlight. So which gully was the right one? I had reset my altimeter at Twin Lakes, so I knew my altitude pretty accurately, but that wasn't enough in this case to pinpoint my position. If I started up the wrong gully, I'd almost certainly waste so much time that I would miss sunrise.

I pulled out my ancient GPS receiver, got a position fix, and plotted my position on my USGS 7.5 minute quad. Then I measured a course off the map from my position to the top of the Red Couloir and identified which notch in the skyline, faintly visible against the stars, had to be the right gully. I started up.

Soon I found evidence that other climbers had passed that way. Either I was in the right gully or a lot of other climbers had made the same mistake I had. At the top of the Red Couloir, I turned left, following the guidebook's description, but in the dark missed the line of cairns indicating the best route. Now neither GPS nor map, compass, and altimeter could help me. I needed to find the easiest route, not navigate. After thrashing up unstable talus and gravel-covered slabs, I reached some broken ledges just beneath the last 100-foot cliff blocking access to the summit ridge. Could I crack the final barrier?

With difficulty I scrambled up to a sharp notch and peered over into the yawning abyss beyond. Surely that couldn't be the easiest way; if it was, I was certainly not going to climb it in hiking boots (rather than technical rock-climbing shoes) with a 4 × 5 field camera on my back. I backed down and tried another way, eventually climbing through a short, steep tunnel behind a huge boulder to gain the summit ridge. I emerged to discover that the summit was just 50 yards away. A few minutes later I was photographing a spectacular sunrise from the roof of the Rockies.

When I wrote the second edition of this book in 1998, handheld GPS receivers for outdoorsmen were an expensive, cumbersome, inaccurate novelty. Today they are vastly improved and in fact ubiquitous. Fishermen are using GPS receivers to navigate through the woods to prime fishing holes located far from any trail. Cross-country skiers are using them to relocate their cars, even when drifting snow has obscured their tracks and low clouds are hiding all landmarks. Backpackers are using them to track their progress on the trail and to relocate their tents at night after lingering on some high overlook to watch the sunset. And mountaineers are using them to navigate across treacherous glaciers when sudden storms produce blinding whiteouts, in which even the ground underfoot seems shifting and uncertain.

Some GPS units now include a two-way radio. These receivers can show you the position of compatible units carried by friends or relatives on a map displayed on your own receiver, as well as send your companions your exact location so they can plot where you are.

Many smartphones now include a GPS chip. With the addition of a suitable GPS app, your smartphone can give you many of the capabilities of a stand-alone GPS receiver.

At least two companies now make emergency locator beacons (ELBs) incorporating GPS technology. ELBs can broadcast an SOS message including your exact position if you encounter a life-threatening emergency in the backcountry and cannot extricate yourself. The message is relayed via satellite to the search-and-rescue team responsible for your area. ELBs work even when cell phones can't. You can also use ELBs to send your position plus an "All's well" message or a message asking friends to come help if, for example, your car broke down on some remote four-wheel-drive road and you don't really need to call out the cavalry.

At the time of writing, one company, DeLorme, even makes a GPS unit that can communicate wirelessly with an ELB. The combination of the two devices lets you type a very short text message on your GPS unit and transmit it wirelessly to the ELB, which in turn beams it up to a satellite. There are also ELBs that can interface with a smartphone, which allows you to send short text messages, including your location, via satellite. The system works when your cell phone, by itself, cannot.

Don't assume, however, that buying an ELB means guaranteed rescue. The user agreement for the Spot ELB states explicitly that sending an SOS does not create a "duty to rescue" in the legal sense if the search-and-rescue leader deems it unfeasible due to terrain or weather. Don't expect a rescue helicopter to swoop down from the sky if you break your leg on the summit of Mt. Everest. Users should also remember that stiff penalties are assessed if you call for a rescue when none is really needed.

The uses of GPS receivers both in the field and in the city go on and on. Athletes are using wristwatch-style GPS units that also include a heart-rate monitor to track the distance they've run or biked, the altitude they've gained and lost, the heart rate they've achieved, and the pace they've maintained. Motorists are using them to navigate unfamiliar cities. Companies of all sizes are using them to track cargo moving by land, air, and sea and even to keep tabs on their employees. The GPS receiver I was using on Sunlight Peak, which I'd purchased in 1998, was a dinosaur compared to the sophisticated receiver I purchased recently. By the time you read this book, even more new and innovative uses of GPS technology will undoubtedly have become available.

GPS technology has even spawned a new sport: geocaching. Geocaching is a kind of modern-day treasure hunt. Players put inexpensive trinkets and a logbook inside some kind of waterproof container, hide the container either in the woods or in the city, then post the GPS coordinates of the geocache online. Other players then use those coordinates to try to find the cache. Once they locate it, they take one of the "treasures" inside and replace it with an item of equal or greater value. After signing the logbook, they put the cache back where they found it, return home, and post a report of their find online.

Kids love treasure hunts, which makes geocaching a great family sport. Today you can even buy simple, inexpensive GPS receivers aimed specifically at children that come preloaded with the coordinates of roughly 250,000 geocaches located across the United States.

As with any sport there are rules, or at least guidelines. This is a family activity; don't put sexually explicit or otherwise potentially offensive items in a geocache. Likewise, don't put weapons, ammunition, drugs, alcohol, or food inside a cache. And don't place geocaches inside national parks or on private land.

As the sport has grown in popularity, it has evolved lots of variants. There are many geocaching sites on the web that can provide additional information and the coordinates of a geocache near you. One of the best sites is www.geocaching.com. A quick search in your favorite search engine will reveal many more.

The Basics of GPS Navigation

The Global Positioning System (GPS) is the most significant advance in navigation since the invention of the compass in the twelfth century. The system was originally created by the US military in the 1970s as a way to help submarines locate their exact position before launching a ballistic missile. The heart of the system is a constellation of twenty-four satellites that orbit the Earth twice a day. Each satellite continuously broadcasts its position and the exact time. At least five satellites are above the horizon at all times, regardless of your position on Earth. The time required for a signal to reach the GPS receiver indicates the distance between the receiver and the satellite. By combining the information received from three or more satellites, a GPS receiver can calculate your exact position in degrees of latitude and longitude or, more usefully, in terms of your UTM coordinates (more on that later). Take that information to a map and you know where you are. GPS receivers use the same satellite signals to provide you with a rough estimate of your altitude. However, a good barometric altimeter, which works off air pressure, is much more accurate if reset frequently at points of known elevation. Some GPS units now include a barometric altimeter.

In the early days of the GPS system, the military deliberately degraded the GPS signals available to consumers to prevent terrorists from taking advantage of them. The policy was called "selective availability." That meant that accuracy was limited to about 100 yards 95 percent of the time. Five percent of the time, the error could be worse. The military reversed itself in May 2000 and dropped its selective availability policy.

In 2003 the Wide Area Augmentation System (WAAS) became available. This network of ground-based stations, as well as two satellites, improves accuracy still further, although not all GPS receivers are "WAAS-enabled." The WAAS system is currently available only in North America, but other countries are developing similar systems. WAAS-enabled receivers can provide accuracy, under ideal circumstances, as good as 10 feet. More commonly, however, you should expect accuracy of about 20 to 30 feet. GPS receivers provide an estimate, in feet, of their accuracy depending on how many satellites they're tracking. Interpret that figure to mean that your true position should lie within a circle with a radius equal to the estimated error. If the error is 30 feet, for example, your true position should be within 30 feet, in any direction, of the position provided by the GPS receiver.

Even an error of 20 or 30 feet is still pretty amazing. Boosters argue that the use of GPS receivers means that nobody should ever get lost again. As astounding as their capabilities are, however, GPS receivers are not infallible substitutes for good map-reading skills, a compass, and a keen awareness of your surroundings. Without batteries they're useless, and any electronic device can malfunction. Cliffs and dense foliage can block the signals from the GPS satellites. If you're in thick woods, you may need to find a clearing in order to get a position fix. If you're in the depths of a slot canyon in southern Utah, you may have to climb out of the canyon—if that's possible—to determine your position. To get the most out of a GPS receiver, it's essential to understand both its tremendous strengths and its weaknesses.

Simple position fixes are only the beginning of a GPS receiver's capabilities. GPS receivers also let you record the position of *waypoints*—any location you want the device to memorize. You can record waypoints as you reach them by turning on the receiver, letting it get a position fix, and then entering that position into the GPS receiver's memory. You can also record waypoints by measuring the coordinates of a waypoint on a map and then entering those coordinates into the receiver along with a name. To make the process still easier, you can now create waypoints by clicking on an electronic map displayed on your home computer, giving your waypoints descriptive names, and then uploading those waypoints to your receiver.

All GPS receivers include a "Go to" feature. Just press the "Go to" or "Find" button, select a waypoint from the list that appears on the receiver's LCD display, and the receiver will tell you the distance to the waypoint and the compass bearing you must follow to reach it.

Let's say a foot of fresh powder snow has just blanketed the high country and there's more in the air. You know the new snow means there will be some great skiing above Powder Lake, but you also know that the fresh snow will have erased all traces of the Powder Lake trail. With a GPS receiver that's no problem. First you use a map to calculate the position of Powder Lake (more on that below). Then you enter that information in the receiver as a waypoint named *Powder Lake.* Next you drive to the trailhead, let the receiver get a position fix, and enter that as a waypoint named *truck.* Then you press "Go to" *Powder Lake.* The receiver tells you the lake is 3 miles away at a bearing of 242 degrees. Following your compass, you ski through the woods to the lake, cut up the powder until your thighs are jelly, and then go exploring north of the lake for several hours. By now the continuing storm has covered your tracks again. How do you get back to your truck? Just press "Go to" *truck* and the receiver will tell you the distance and compass bearing you must follow to reach your vehicle.

GPS receivers also allow you to create *routes* when it's impractical to make a direct beeline toward your destination. For example, you could record the position of your truck and then record a series of waypoints as you head out for a day of ski touring. Logical waypoints might include a major stream crossing, a lake, a small meadow with a distinctive dead snag, and a saddle a half mile below the summit. To find your way back to your truck after lunch, you can create a route from your position (the summit) through each waypoint in turn, ending at your truck. The GPS receiver will guide you by providing the distance and compass bearing to the next waypoint. When you reach a waypoint, the receiver automatically switches to the next waypoint in sequence, providing the distance and bearing to it until you reach your vehicle again. Figure 7-1 shows the waypoints I created during a recent hike in the Fiery Furnace in Arches National Park.

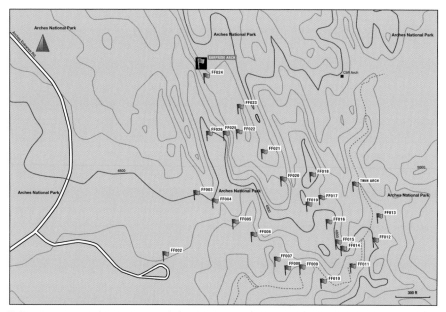

7-1 This illustration, based on a screenshot from Garmin's Basecamp mapping software, shows the waypoints I recorded while hiking in the Fiery Furnace, a mazelike region of sandstone fins, towers, and canyons in Arches National Park.

You can also create a route at home by entering the coordinates of the various waypoints you expect to pass on the way to your destination. Most mapping software today lets you string together waypoints you've placed on the electronic map into a route, then upload the completed route to your GPS receiver.

GPS receivers have another useful feature: the ability to create a *track*, which is a continuous string of waypoints created automatically as you travel. See figure 7-2 to see the track I created during my Fiery Furnace hike. You can specify, in various ways, how often the receiver creates a waypoint. Should you need to reverse your route, you can tell the receiver to guide you home. It will provide the direction you must travel to retrace your steps until you reach your starting point. With many receivers you can save your track, then download it to your computer and plot it on an electronic map or on satellite photos provided by Google Earth so you can see exactly how lost you really were. Note that using the tracking feature means the receiver must be on continuously, which of course burns up batteries.

Continuously tracking your position also means you can get real-time information on exactly how far you've hiked, including all the twists and turns

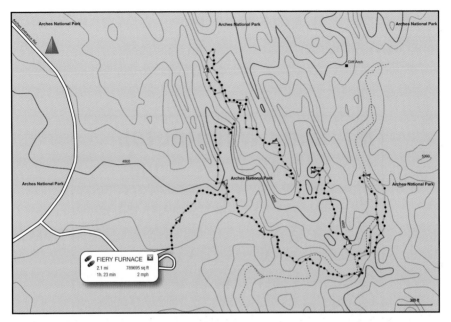

7-2 This illustration, based on a screen shot from Garmin's Basecamp mapping software, shows the track my receiver recorded while I hiked in the Fiery Furnace, an intricate region of sandstone fins, towers, and canyons in Arches National Park.

of the trail. This is a different measurement from doing a "Go to" back to your truck or campsite, which only gives you a straight-line, as-the-crow-flies distance.

Buying a GPS Receiver

Today you can find GPS receivers for well under $100 as well as units costing nearly ten times as much. With such a wide range of receivers available, you need to narrow your options by deciding which features you need and which features you can do without.

All handheld GPS units will give you a position fix and allow you to create waypoints as well as basic routes and tracks. As the cost goes up, so does the number of waypoints, routes, and tracks you can record before the receiver runs out of memory. Inexpensive units have a small, grayscale screen; better ones have larger, color displays. As cost goes up, so do the speed of the processor and the sensitivity of the antenna. Those features combine to give you a faster "time to first fix" and better ability to track your position while in the forest, where foliage can block the satellite signals. Better units will have longer battery life and the ability to add extra storage by purchasing a memory card such as an SD or Micro-SD card.

Another basic divide is between receivers that are capable of displaying maps and those that are not. Mapping receivers plot your position on a topographic map that is displayed on the screen, as in figure 7-3. That can help you identify

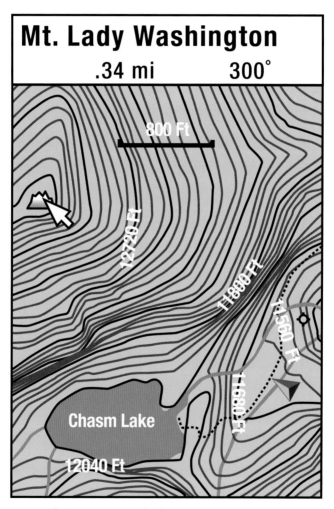

7-3 This illustration, based on a screen shot from the map screen on a Garmin GPSMAP 62s, shows Chasm Lake in Rocky Mountain National Park. At the left side of the screen, the white arrow (the cursor) points to a landmark; at the top of the screen, you can see that the landmark is a peak called Mt. Lady Washington. The blue triangle represents your current position. Data at the top of the screen show you the distance and direction from your position to the cursor, which in this case points to Mt. Lady Washington.

your location more quickly. Most mapping receivers come with a basic, small-scale map built in. You can purchase more detailed maps of specific areas and upload them to your receiver, including topographic maps with approximately the same level of detail as a USGS 7.5 minute quad. Various websites also offer free maps of some areas that are compatible with specific receivers.

Before you get too excited about this feature, however, remember that the screens on even very good GPS units are only 1.5 × 2.5 inches or so. That's much smaller than a full-size 7.5 minute quad, so it's difficult to get a feel for the broad picture, although you can zoom in and out on the map. Place names may not display on the map until you position your cursor over an icon. Also note that the topographic data are highly compressed, which tends to smooth out the subtle wrinkles in the contours that tell the observant eye where cliff bands are lurking. A paper USGS 7.5 minute quad is still the gold standard for topographic maps, and I never attempt to navigate through challenging terrain without one.

Some of the latest GPS receivers come with touch screens reminiscent of those found on some smartphones. These interfaces are very fast to use, particularly when you're typing in the name of a waypoint, track, or route, since you can tap the screen to enter a letter rather than using arrow keys to scroll to each letter and then pressing "Enter." However, most current-generation touch screens are harder to see in bright sunlight than conventional screens; some work poorly or not at all with gloves on. Before buying a touch-screen GPS receiver, examine the screen in direct sunlight and try working the controls with gloves on.

You can now buy GPS receivers that include an electronic compass, an altimeter, and even a digital camera. The camera I can live without, since I almost always have a full-size DSLR (digital single lens reflex) with me in the backcountry. The altimeter can be very useful, although resetting it at points of known elevation can be more cumbersome than resetting a wristwatch-style altimeter. On my high-end receiver, you have to punch in each digit of the elevation one by one. On my wristwatch barometric altimeter, you press one button for two seconds to enter the "reference elevation" mode, then press either the up or down button until the altimeter reads out the correct elevation—a much simpler system. Electronic compasses are a convenience, but even the best have a tendency to wander a bit before pointing you in the right direction to reach the next waypoint. That's particularly true as you close in on the next waypoint. GPS receivers are also not designed as devices for sighting bearings. None can be used as a protractor to measure a course on a map. I always carry a mirror-sight compass to accurately measure bearings in the field and courses on the map. Figure 7-4 shows a typical GPS compass display.

Some units also include lots of other bells and whistles, such as a calculator, calendar, alarm clock, sunrise/sunset and moonrise/moonset almanac, and an

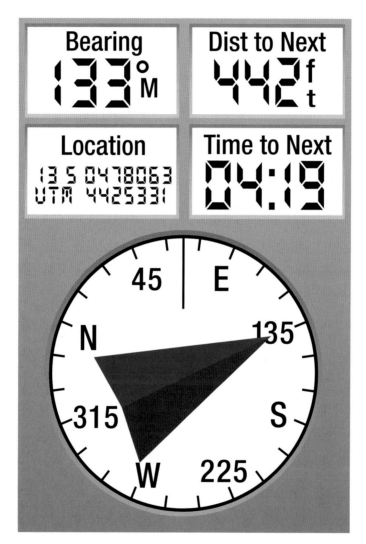

7-4 This illustration, based on a screenshot from a Garmin GPSMAP 62s, shows a fairly typical compass screen. At the top of the screen, you can see the distance and bearing to the next landmark, your current position in UTM coordinates, and the device's estimate of when you will arrive at the next waypoint. The direction arrow on the compass also points at the next waypoint.

estimate of the best times for hunting and fishing. Some can even display an elevation profile of your journey. One of the most useful features is a trip computer, which can show you the exact distance you've hiked if you turn on your GPS receiver at the trailhead, as well as a host of other data (see figure 7-5). I'll let you decide which of those features, if any, would be useful to you.

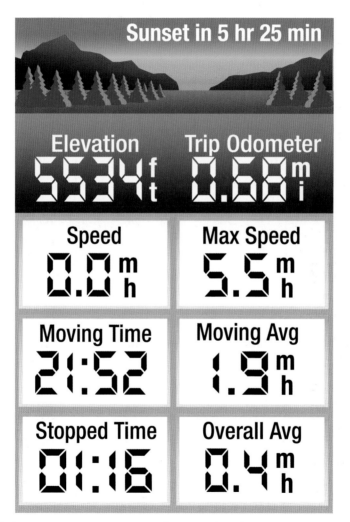

7-5 A typical trip-computer screen gives you information about the distance you've traveled and your time en route. This illustration is based on the trip-computer screen on a Garmin GPSMAP 62s.

Using a GPS Receiver in the Field

Your strategy for using your GPS receiver in the field can range from simple to complex. At a minimum you should record a waypoint at the trailhead if you're day-hiking or at your campsite if you're backpacking. After all, one primary purpose for owning a GPS unit is to sleep warm at night in your own bed or sleeping bag, instead of shivering all night while huddled under a rock in a menacing gale.

The next step upward in complexity is to record waypoints at key locations along your route, such as the must-find bridge across a big creek and the point where the trail leaves the trees and climbs above timberline. Down in dense timber your snowshoe or ski tracks will remain visible for quite a while, even if it's windy and snowing. Above timberline they can vanish in an hour or less. When I climbed 14,433-foot Mt. Elbert, the highest peak in Colorado, in January and shot moonrise at sunset from the summit, I was worried about finding my way down in the dark. I created a waypoint at my campsite, another where the trail first emerged from continuous forest, and a third at the highest trees. I also reset my wristwatch altimeter regularly and kept track of my position on my 7.5 minute USGS quad. As it turned out, the night was calm, the full moon was shining brightly, and I was able to navigate simply by sight while descending the windblown tundra to a saddle. When the snowpack deepened, I picked up my snowshoe tracks and followed them down to my tent. But it could easily have been much different, and having the waypoints recorded certainly relieved my worries.

Let's say your route is complicated, with little margin for error. Perhaps you're weaving upward through cliff bands as you climb out of a canyon in Utah. In a typical scenario you might start up through a break in a cliff band and then need to traverse a quarter mile left or right to find the break in the next cliff band. Once you've climbed through that, you traverse again to the next break in the next cliff. Recording a waypoint at your starting point is important but doesn't solve the problem, since a straight-line path back to your car will lead you over multiple cliff bands. You could record a waypoint at the top and bottom of each break in each cliff band, or you could simply turn on your receiver when you leave your vehicle and let it record a track. When the time comes to retrace your steps, you can navigate from one waypoint to the next or let the backtracking feature on your GPS receiver guide you home.

Remember that running your receiver continuously uses batteries quickly. Most modern receivers get twelve to twenty hours from one set. While that's plenty for an average day of hiking, you should always carry at least one spare set, just in case.

Which is better for finding your way home, using waypoints or just using the backtrack feature? Here are some things you should know.

Using the backtrack feature on your GPS receiver is so simple it sometimes becomes simpleminded. As a general rule the backtrack feature will direct you to retrace your steps exactly. Let's say you're hiking up a trail to a pass and decide to make a short out-and-back detour on a spur trail that leads to a nearby lake. After returning to the main trail, you continue to the pass and enable the backtracking feature. Your GPS will direct you to take the same detour out to the lake and back that you took on the way up. If you bypass the detour and continue straight down the main trail, your GPS receiver will tell you to turn around and go back to the junction of the main trail and the spur trail. If you persist in ignoring its recommendations, it should eventually wake up and smell the waypoints and begin directing you to continue down along your ascent route. In whiteout conditions, however, things could still get pretty confusing.

Some backtrack displays only provide a compass bearing and distance to your final destination, not to the next twist and turn in your route home. You have to follow the direction arrow displayed on the screen, which may not be as accurate as following a course measured with a mirror-sight compass. If your track records waypoints frequently, they will be quite close together. If you have some slight inaccuracies in each position fix and the next waypoint is close at hand, the compass bearing from one to the next may be inaccurate. You can actually get a more precise direction from one waypoint to the next if they are a bit farther apart, because that minimizes the effect of errors in each position fix.

One advantage of recording waypoints instead of a track, therefore, is that you can choose which waypoint to navigate to next, and so take the most efficient route home. Let's say you hike up to series of large meadows and spend the day wandering around looking for flowers to photograph. When the time comes to head home, you don't want to retrace all your wanderings before leaving the meadow and heading back down through the woods. Having a simple waypoint at the edge of the forest means you can go straight there and immediately begin the hike out without wasting time.

There are, of course, solutions to the limitations of the backtrack feature. In the example above, you could turn off the track-recording feature on your GPS receiver once you reach the meadow so you have a clean track from the edge of the meadow back to your vehicle when you need it.

Here's another example of the limitations of the backtrack feature. Let's say you're hiking a loop. You've come 7 miles already and are 85 percent of the way around the loop, but you're having difficulty figuring out the best route over the last mile. The backtrack feature on your GPS receiver can only lead you back the way you came—7 long miles. You're better off to tell the GPS receiver to navigate to your car, plot your position on a detailed map, and then carefully study your map to determine what obstacles, if any, lie between your current position and your vehicle. I'll talk more about plotting your position on a map in just a bit.

One final caveat about backtracking: Don't try to use a GPS receiver loaded with backcountry maps to backtrack when driving. Modern GPS receivers are so accurate that they actually create problems when trying to retrace your route on the highway. For example, I recently ran an errand that took me north on Foothills Parkway, a four-lane road. After turning onto Arapaho Avenue and completing my errand, I engaged the backtrack feature. Following the GPS receiver's guidance, I returned to the intersection of Foothills Parkway and Arapaho and turned south. The GPS immediately showed me, with its direction arrow, that I should turn around, head *north* in the *southbound* lanes, make a U-turn, and head *south* in the *northbound* lanes in order to retrace my route exactly. My southbound route was only 75 feet west of my northbound route, but that was enough for the GPS receiver to conclude I was not retracing my steps exactly. If I had been weaving through cliff bands interspersed with narrow ledges, I would have greatly appreciated the precision. Since following the GPS unit's directions would have been suicidal on the highway, I cheerfully ignored the insistent direction arrow and drove home safely. If you want to navigate in the city, buy a package of city maps designed for highway navigation and load it onto your GPS receiver.

For all the reasons described above, my preferred strategy is to record waypoints at each significant location along my route, so I can choose which waypoint to navigate to next and so I can get an accurate direction and distance to the next waypoint. If the route-finding is critical, I'll transfer the bearing provided by my GPS receiver to my mirror-sight compass so I can walk the course with the greatest possible accuracy. If I've got plenty of battery power, however, I'll still leave the GPS on continuously so I can use the trip log to tell me how many miles I've walked. I record the track so I can download it to my computer after the trip. For starters, it can be fun to see exactly where you've been. You can also turn your track into a route, which you can then upload to your GPS receiver if you want to repeat the trip. If you hike a trail in the summer, for example, your track would record the path the trail takes through the forest. If you create a route from your track, then return in the winter, it will be easier to find the summer trail-cut even if the trail itself is buried under 3 feet of snow. That could mean a lot less bushwhacking.

It's a good idea to download all your tracks, waypoints, and routes from your GPS receiver after each trip and save them on your desktop computer, and then delete them from your receiver. When you're in the field, you'll then have a clean receiver, which makes adding waypoints very fast. On my receiver I need to push only two buttons to create a waypoint if I accept the default name, which I can do if there are no other waypoints with similar names on the receiver.

Whichever way you choose, retracing a track or navigating to waypoints, don't let the GPS receiver lull you into a sense of complacency. Maintain your "situational awareness," as the search-and-rescue folks like to call it. Pay attention to what each break in a cliff band looks like as you climb up it. When you reach the top of the break, *before proceeding onward,* look back down it and really study it. Memorize some distinctive landmark: a bright orange splash of lichen, a fallen tree with a twisted limb, the way a slab of sandstone leans up against an adjacent boulder. After all, it's conceivable you could drop your GPS receiver over one of those cliffs; you can't drop your head.

Creating a Route before Leaving Home

If you're anticipating really difficult route-finding—off-trail, in the dark, in the winter in remote areas where there will be no tracks—and if you can identify the best route from the map, then you may want to create a route and either type it in or upload it to your GPS receiver before leaving home.

Before we dive into the best ways to create routes on a map, paper or electronic, we need to talk again about map datums. I mentioned the topic in the chapter on maps, but it bears repeating here.

Topographic maps are built on a "datum," which is basically the reference point for the coordinate system used to plot map data, plus, usually, some kind of mathematical model of the Earth. We don't need to get into all the technical details here, but you do need to know this: Different maps use different datums. Since you can't change the datum of an existing paper map, you must set your receiver, and your electronic maps, to match the datum of the paper map you'll have with you in the field. Failure to do this can make a GPS position you plot on your map be inaccurate by several hundred yards. The datum each USGS map uses is printed in the lower-left corner. Many USGS 7.5 minute quads use NAD 27, which is short for North American Datum 1927. Computerized maps may by default use NAD 83, the North American Datum of 1983, or WGS 84 (World Geodetic System of 1984), which is essentially identical to NAD 83. Most GPS receivers use WGS 84 by default, so you'll need to change that before you start plotting positions on a map that uses NAD 27.

The easiest way, by far, to create a route at home is to purchase a detailed electronic map that covers the area you'll be visiting. As I described in more detail in Chapter 1, creating waypoints can be as simple as clicking once on the map.

With some software you can also draw a route on the map with your mouse and then have the software automatically place waypoints along its length, by using a distance between waypoints that you specify, by placing a specified number of waypoints along the length of the route, or by letting the software assign waypoints at what it deems to be critical turns. Once you have created all the waypoints, the software can easily create a route incorporating those waypoints. You can then plug your receiver into your computer with a serial cable or USB cable and upload your new route.

For example, on a recent family vacation in Moab, Utah, we decided to hike to Tukuhnikivats Arch. I'd seen dramatic photos of the arch perched atop a sandstone ridge with the snow-capped La Sal Mountains in the background, so it seemed like a worthy objective. I started by opening an electronic map of the area on my laptop computer. I then created a series of waypoints at each significant junction in the maze of dirt roads leading to the trailhead. Then I created a waypoint for the arch itself using coordinates provided by a guidebook. Figure 7-6 shows the route I created. The arch itself is not marked even on the paper USGS 7.5 minute quad of the area.

When we started driving, my wife Cora let me know as we approached each turn, which was a good thing, since more roads existed on the ground than were marked on the map. Once we started hiking, I told the GPS receiver to navigate to the arch. After half a mile we spotted it in the distance, then lost sight of it again behind foreground cliff bands. The GPS receiver kept pointing us in the right direction, however, as we climbed steeply past cliffs and sandstone slabs. At last we emerged onto the ridge and saw only a small sandstone fin where the arch should be. At first I was puzzled; then, a few steps later, we all had to laugh. Contained within the fin was the arch, all right, but in contrast to the impressive arch of my imagination, the opening in the real arch was only 5 feet high. We immediately rechristened it "Daddy's Wild Goose Chase Arch," shot a few photos, and hiked back the way we came. The coordinates of the arch given in the guidebook, by the way, were off by a couple of hundred feet when plotted on the USGS 7.5 minute quad of the area, perhaps because the guidebook author was using his GPS receiver's default map datum (he didn't specify, but it was probably WGS 84), while the Kane Springs USGS 7.5 minute quad uses NAD 27.

If you don't own electronic maps or you're in the field and want to create a new waypoint, you have two choices. If you have a mapping receiver, you may be able to create a new waypoint by positioning a cursor on the device's map and then recording that position. You may also be able to search for a

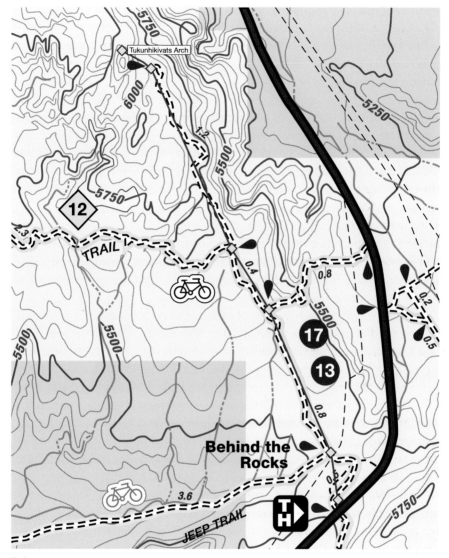

7-6 This illustration shows the route I created to find Tukuhnikivats Arch, near Moab, Utah. The yellow diamonds are the waypoints I created.

geographic feature by typing in its name, moving the cursor to that feature, and then creating a waypoint at that location.

If your receiver doesn't have that feature, you'll have to determine the coordinates by measuring them on the map. Once you've entered the coordinates in your GPS receiver as a waypoint, you can press "Go to," select your new waypoint, and know both its bearing and how far away it is—which is not necessarily the same thing as knowing the best route to take to reach it. You can also create a series of waypoints using either method and then string them together into a route while sitting there in your tent.

Virtually all maps, including the highway maps you can buy at every gas station, have latitude and longitude marked off in the margins. And it's true you can set your receiver to read out your position in degrees of latitude and longitude. Frankly, using latitude and longitude to plot your position on a map is a pain. The better way is to use the UTM system, which I'll describe below. Since not all maps show this coordinate system, however, I'll spend a few minutes describing how to use longitude and latitude.

First, a refresher from fifth-grade geography. Lines of latitude run parallel to the equator. The equator is at latitude zero degrees; the poles are at latitude 90 degrees north and south. Lines of latitude are often called parallels. One degree of latitude equals about 69 miles.

Lines of longitude run perpendicular to the equator and extend to the North and South Poles. By convention, the line of zero degrees longitude, which is called the prime meridian, runs through Greenwich, England. Longitude is measured in degrees east and west of the prime meridian, up to 180 degrees. One degree of longitude equals about 69 miles at the equator, but the distance between meridians decreases as you approach the poles, where all lines of longitude converge.

By convention, 1 degree of both latitude and longitude is divided into 60 minutes. Each minute is further divided into 60 seconds.

As you're probably starting to realize, measuring the exact latitude and longitude of a waypoint on a map is much more of a hassle than it sounds. Here's the easiest way: Start by using a ruler or other straightedge to draw a line from the waypoint to the right or left edge of the map (whichever is closest). We'll call this the *latitude line*. Draw a second line to the top or bottom edge of the map. We'll call this the *longitude line*. The lines should be perpendicular to the edges of the map. Most maps have the latitude and longitude marked at intervals along the borders. By noting where your latitude and longitude lines intersect the borders of your map, you can eyeball an approximate set of coordinates for your waypoint.

To determine these coordinates accurately, however, you have to figure out a latitude scale: the number of minutes of latitude that corresponds to 1 inch on the map. For example, let's say that the distance between 39 degrees, 52 minutes north latitude and 39 degrees, 53 minutes north latitude is 2 inches on your map. That's 2 inches per minute of latitude, or 1 inch for 0.5 minute. If the latitude line of your waypoint is 1 inch north of the 54-minute mark on the border of your map, its latitude is 39 degrees, 54 minutes, 30 seconds. On a 7.5 minute USGS quad, 1 inch on the map equals about 0.33 minute or 20 seconds of latitude. To determine the longitude accurately, you have to figure out a second scale for the number of minutes of longitude that correspond to 1 inch on that particular map. The latitude and longitude scales are not the same because the distance between two lines of longitude varies depending on your latitude. Once established, the longitude scale remains the same for maps at the same latitude but would not be the same for maps of areas a few hundred miles north or south. Figuring out the exact longitude and latitude of a point on the map is most easily done in the warmth of your home, with a flat place to lay out the map, a yardstick, a pocket calculator, and plenty of head-scratching time.

The UTM Coordinate System

Fortunately it's much easier to calculate the coordinates of a waypoint when using Universal Transverse Mercator (UTM) coordinates, which all modern GPS receivers can handle. Before you throw up your hands in horror at the thought of learning a whole new coordinate system, read the next few paragraphs. The system is simpler than its arcane name implies and in fact is more intuitive than latitude and longitude for use in the field.

The UTM coordinate system is a metric grid system covering all of the Earth except areas near the poles. Its basic unit is a long, narrow strip of the Earth called a zone. These strips run vertically. Each zone is 6 degrees wide, so it takes sixty

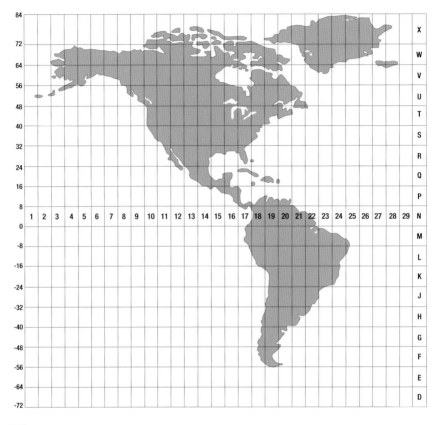

7-7 The UTM coordinate system divides most of the earth, except the polar regions, into 60 zones, each 6 degrees of longitude wide and numbered 1 through 60. The earth is further subdivided into 24 horizontal bands, each given a letter designation.

zones to cover the entire Earth (see figure 7-7). Zones are numbered 1 through 60, starting at the 180th meridian and counting eastward. Zones 10 through 19 cover the United States (see figure 7-8).

The Earth is also divided into horizontal bands, starting at 80 degrees south latitude and extending to 84 degrees north latitude. These bands are given letter designations, starting at C in the south and extending to X in the north. The letters O and I are not used, to avoid confusion with zero and 1. All bands except X are 8 degrees high; X is 12 degrees high. The bands designated S and T cover most of the United States. Displaying your UTM coordinates on your GPS receiver can be confusing if you happen to be in the S band. The coordinate readout will give you your vertical zone first (a two-digit designation, like 13, which covers most of Colorado) and then the letter S, representing your band. The letter S does not stand for south, as in south of the equator the way you would designate a Southern Hemisphere latitude, nor should it be confused with a 5. The UTM coordinates of Tukuhnikivats Arch, for example, using the NAD 27 map datum, are:

12 S 635061
4257196

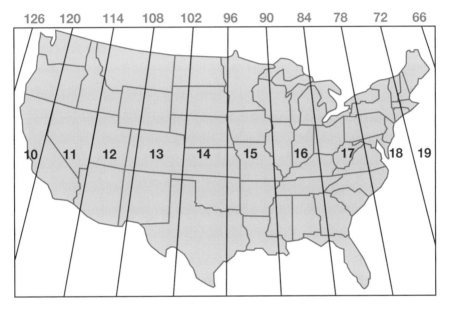

7-8 The United States lies within UTM zones 10 through 19, labeled in red in this illustration. In addition, most of the United States lies within the horizontal bands given the UTM designators S and T (not marked on this map). Lines of longitude are labeled in blue across the top of the illustration.

Now let's demystify the rest of those numbers.

Your position in UTM coordinates is defined first by the zone you're in. Your position inside each zone is then defined by your distance, in meters, east and north of the origin, which is the lower-left (southwest) corner of your zone. Here's the tricky part. Unlike the Cartesian coordinate system used in mathematics, the origin is *not* defined as point zero, zero. Instead, the central meridian of the zone is defined arbitrarily as having a value of 500,000 meters east even though it isn't actually 500,000 meters east of the origin. The east value (or "easting") of the origin is therefore given as 500,000 minus the actual distance to the origin from the central meridian of the zone. In other words, let's say the western boundary of your zone happens to be 300,000 meters west of the zone's central meridian. The easting value at the western boundary of your zone is 200,000 (500,000 − 300,000 = 200,000), not zero.

The easting value of the origin in every zone at the equator, for example, is approximately 160,000 meters, not zero. At 84 degrees north the easting value at the origin is about 465,000 meters, not zero.

The north value of the origin is much easier to understand. For the Northern Hemisphere it's simply the distance, in meters, from the equator to the southern boundary of your zone. In the Southern Hemisphere the equator is assigned a value of 10,000,000 meters. The northing of the origin of each southern zone is calculated from that figure.

Why this apparently arcane system? It dispenses with the problem of the distance between lines of longitude becoming progressively smaller as you move closer to the poles and prevents the use of any negative numbers.

Fortunately actually using UTM coordinates is a lot simpler than explaining where the numbers come from. Just think of your easting as the number of meters east of the origin (the lower-left or southwest corner of your zone) and the northing as the number of meters north of the origin. You don't have to worry about the fact that the easting and northing of the origin are not zero.

The legend on most large- and intermediate-scale USGS topos will tell you your UTM zone. Along the borders of the map, you'll find short blue lines set at 1,000-meter intervals. These blue lines are referred to as *1,000-meter grid ticks*. Each tick on the right and left sides of the map is labeled with the northing of that point, expressed in meters. Each tick on the top and bottom sides of the map is labeled with the easting of that point, again expressed in meters.

For the sake of simplicity in reading the map, the last three zeros of the number are eliminated except in the tick marks near the bottom-right and top-left corners of the map. To further simplify map reading, the first one or two numbers of the northing and easting are printed in small type, as typically they are a constant over one map sheet. The grid tick labeled 474 on the bottom edge of the map, for instance, has an easting of 474,000 meters. The grid tick labeled 3719 on the right edge of the map has a northing of 3,719,000 meters. You'll notice that all I've done to convert an abbreviated grid tick number to meters is add three zeros and place the commas in the appropriate places. Note also that a difference of 1 between two abbreviated grid tick numbers equals 1,000 meters. The distance between grid ticks 474 and 475, for example, is 1,000 meters.

One beauty of the UTM system is that the units are intelligible. If someone told you that you had to walk 2 minutes of latitude north to reach your house, you'd probably have no idea if you would be home in an hour or a week. (You're actually just over a mile from home.) On the other hand, if someone tells you that you have to walk 1,000 meters (1 kilometer, or about 0.6 mile), you know you probably should be there in less than twenty minutes. If you set your GPS receiver to give you your position in UTM coordinates, you can watch the meter turn (literally) as you walk. Your position, as expressed in meters, will change with every few strides. Another beauty of the UTM system is that the scale is always the same for both northing and easting, unlike latitude and longitude, which have separate scales.

Some of the most recent large-scale topographic maps will have a UTM coordinate grid printed on the map. Most USGS 7.5 minute quads, however, do not. For those maps the first step in measuring the UTM coordinates of a waypoint is to use a yardstick and a pen to draw lines connecting the grid ticks on the map borders so that you have a visible UTM grid. Now, using a ruler—either a conventional 12-incher if you're at home or the one on the edge of your compass—measure the distance from your waypoint to the closest grid tick line to the west. Transfer that measurement to the kilometer scale at the bottom of the map. A kilometer is 1,000 meters; smaller divisions on the kilometer scale represent 100 meters. On a 1:24,000-scale map (the scale used on standard 7.5 minute USGS quads), 1 inch equals 610 meters. If your waypoint is a half inch east of the nearest grid tick line, you know to add 305 meters to the easting of that line. Use the same technique to determine the northing of your waypoint, and you know your waypoint's UTM coordinates.

Find using a ruler cumbersome? There's an easier way. At least one company sells a handy UTM locator grid that consists of a transparent sheet of plastic with a UTM grid marked in black, designed for use with USGS 7.5 minute topos at the 1:24,000 scale. One square on the grid represents 100 meters. You use the transparent UTM grid to determine the distance, in meters, from your prospective waypoint to the first grid tick line to the west and the first grid tick line to the south. For example, let's say you're in zone 13 and the nearest line to the west is labeled 286, meaning that line is assigned an easting of 286,000 meters. The nearest line to the south is labeled 4157, meaning that line is 4,157,000 meters north of the equator. By placing the bottom-left corner of the transparent card's grid on the intersection of those two lines, you can see that the position of the waypoint you're measuring is 700 meters east and 300 meters north of the intersection, as shown in figure 7-9. In the UTM coordinate system, that puts you at 13 S 286700 east, 4157300 north—zone 13, band S, 286,700 meters easting, 4,157,300 meters northing.

USGS 7 1/2-Minute Topographic
Map: Emerald Lake Quadrangle

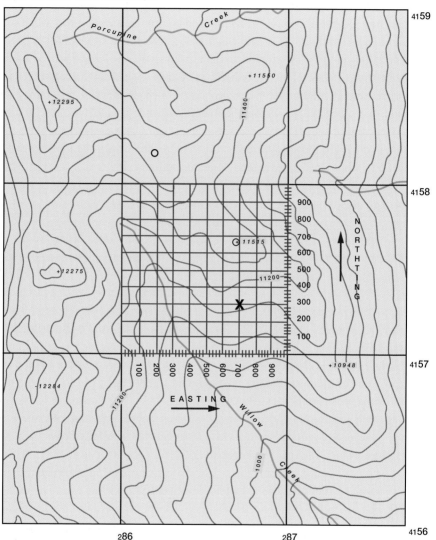

7-9 Let's say you want to know the UTM coordinates of the X marked on the map so you can enter them into your GPS receiver. First, look at the bottom of the map to determine the easting of the first UTM grid line west of the X. It's marked 286. Then look at the right margin of the map to determine the northing of the first UTM grid line south of the X. It's marked 4157. Now position the UTM card with the lower left corner of the grid on the intersection of those two UTM grid lines, as shown. The X is 700 meters east of the 286 grid line and 300 meters north of the 4157 grid line. You know from the legend on the map that this quadrangle lies within zone 13 S. The UTM coordinates of the X are 13 S 286700 , 4157300—zone 13, band S, 286,700 meters easting, 4,157,300 meters northing.

Some compasses now include a similar grid inscribed on the clear plastic base. I find this type of UTM locator grid very helpful, although you use it in a slightly different way. Start by placing the top-right corner of the UTM locator grid on the top-right corner of the 1,000-meter square containing the landmark for which you need coordinates. Now slide the compass down and left (west and south) until the top-right corner of the UTM locator grid sits atop the landmark of interest. Read off the distance in meters along the top and right edges of the UTM locator grid, and add that distance to the values for the bottom-left corner of the 1,000-meter square containing your landmark. Figure 7-10 should make all this clear.

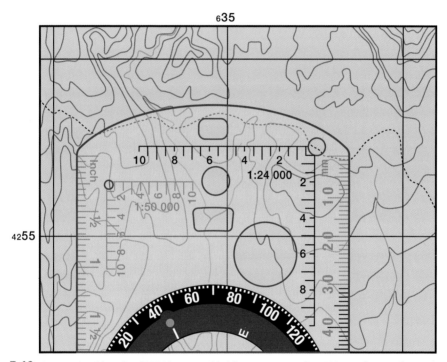

7-10. You can use this style of UTM locator grid either to measure the UTM coordinates of a landmark on the map or to plot your position once you've gotten a position fix from your GPS receiver. In this example, let's say your GPS receiver has given your position on the trail as 12 S 635500 easting, 4255500 northing, and you want to plot your position on your map. You plot your position in two steps: First, place the top-right corner of the UTM locator grid on the top-right corner of the 1,000-meter square that has the 635 easting line as its left border and the 4255 northing line as its bottom border. Second, slide the compass down and left (west and south) across the map until the 500-meter mark on the UTM locator grid's horizontal axis intersects the left border of your square and the 500-meter mark on the UTM locator grid's vertical axis intersects the bottom border of your square. Your position is at the top-right corner of the UTM locator grid. You can mark your position with a pencil pushed through the hole at the top-right corner of the grid.

Once you've determined the UTM coordinates of your destination, you can enter them into your GPS receiver as a waypoint. Press "Go to," select the new waypoint you just created, and the GPS receiver will give you the distance and bearing of your destination.

The same techniques apply when your receiver has given you your position and you need to plot that position on your map to see where you are.

Final Thoughts on GPS Receivers

Do you really *need* a GPS receiver? In the summer probably not, especially if you stick to well-marked trails. During that time of year, a map and compass and perhaps an altimeter are the only navigational tools you really need. If you like to travel cross-country in the summer, you may find a GPS receiver handy once in a while. Remember, however, that summertime cross-country navigating is usually most difficult below timberline, when trees obscure your view of landmarks—a situation in which GPS receivers are less than completely reliable.

If you do a lot of winter travel in the snowy ranges or travel at any time of year in glaciated ranges, you may find a GPS receiver valuable indeed. If the people on the hapless University of Idaho expedition to Mt. McKinley that I described in Chapter 5 had had a GPS receiver (and had remembered to mark their campsite as a waypoint!), they could have easily navigated back to their tents regardless of the weather and spent a comfortable night there instead of spending it shivering and hungry in a snow cave.

GPS receivers are like the many other electronic gizmos that enhance (or is it rule?) our lives. If you use them constantly, they can be extremely useful and a lot of fun. If you don't use them a lot, however, you can easily forget how to use them, and they'll drive you nuts. GPS receivers are not difficult to learn to use, but mastering them does take a little practice. Be prepared to spend several hours working with a new receiver before you take it into the field. If you haven't used your receiver since last summer, throw in the instruction book as well.

After years of carrying my old, clunky GPS receiver only when I felt I really needed it (and sometimes regretting it when I didn't bring it!), I finally bought a modern, top-of-the-line unit. I now carry my GPS receiver even when I don't think it's essential. I like knowing how many miles I've hiked and how many miles I have yet to go. I like being able to download tracks and waypoints to an electronic map after the trip. I like being able to create routes on an electronic map, then upload them to my receiver. And I want to stay in practice with it, so that when I'm climbing a Fourteener in the dark and really need it, I'll know exactly how to pinpoint my position and find my way to the summit before sunrise.

The Sport of Orienteering

Some people no sooner master a skill than they feel a need to test their mastery in competition with others. When people with that disposition combined map-and-compass skills with cross-country running, the sport of orienteering was born.

It began in Scandinavian countries in the late 1800s as a training exercise for military officers. The first orienteering competitions open to the public were held in Norway and Sweden in the 1890s. The sport came to the United States in the 1940s but didn't start to become popular until the 1960s. Today US orienteering clubs stage hundreds of local meets each year. Competitors gather for another twenty-five or so regional and national events as well. In Sweden, Norway, and other European countries, orienteering is a national pastime. A single big meet in Sweden can pull in as many as 15,000 enthusiasts.

In the most popular form of orienteering, competitors must find, in correct order, a series of five to fifteen control points hidden in the woods. An orange-and-white, prism-shaped structure made of fabric or cardboard marks the control point. The controls, as they are called, are either marked on the map furnished to each participant at the start of the race or copied by the participant from a master map after the starting gun sounds. The winner is the runner who finishes in the shortest time after locating all the controls. Runners who miss a control are disqualified. Easy courses may be only 1 or 2 miles long; expert-level courses can stretch 6 miles or longer. The difficulty of the terrain, and hence the time required to finish the course, can vary dramatically, however, so the length of courses can also be specified by the "expected winning time," the time a runner with a rank of 100 in the Orienteering USA ranking system would be expected to take. The expected winning time for a "sprint" race might be twelve to fifteen minutes; the expected winning time for long-course races might be closer to one hundred minutes.

Variations on orienteering have proliferated. At some meets, rather than traveling on foot, orienteers use mountain bikes or skis or even canoes. Some orienteering competitions include relay races. Another popular variation is called score orienteering, sometimes referred to as "score O." Here the goal is to find as many controls as possible in a set period of time rather than to find them in a specific order. More distant controls, in more difficult terrain, often earn competitors more points than closer, easier-to-find controls. A penalty point is assessed if you return late to the starting point, so the game involves strategy as well as route-finding and endurance: Can you find one more control and still make it back to the starting line before time is up? The endurance form of score orienteering, called a Rogaine, can last twenty-four hours. The odd name comes from a mashup of the early boosters' first names, Rod, Gail, and Neil Phillips, although some people claim it stands for Rugged Outdoor Group Activity Involving Navigation and Endurance.

Orienteering maps (see figure 8-1) are usually drawn to a larger scale than standard USGS topos. A scale of 1:10,000 or 1:15,000 is common. The top of the map always represents magnetic north instead of geographic north, so there's no need to worry about correcting for declination. Meet officials field-check each

8-1. Orienteering maps are typically drawn to a much larger scale than USGS 7.5 minute quads. They are also much more detailed and are printed in five colors. Brown indicates landforms. Black is used for rock and man-made features. As on USGS maps, blue is used for water. White indicates open forest, easy to run through. Green is denser forest; the darker the green, the harder the forest is to penetrate. Yellow (think sunshine) indicates open areas. Green vertical stripes are used to indicate undergrowth (slow or difficult running) but otherwise with good visibility.

map as they plot the course and place the controls. They delete trails that have vanished, mark any new ones, and add the details that are one key to finding the controls: fences, boulders, knolls, tiny streams that would escape the USGS's notice. In addition to the map, runners get a very brief description of the terrain feature at which each control point will be found.

Classic orienteering races always use a staggered start, so runners can't simply follow each other from control to control. Ideally the controls are also placed so runners approaching a particular control get no clues from others leaving it. Score O races, including Rogaines, often use a mass start because competitors tend to fan out as they follow their own unique strategy for locating controls and accumulating points.

Only in beginner's races will a straight-line compass course ever be the fastest way from one control to the next. Victory doesn't necessarily go to the fastest runner. Instead it goes to the competitor who can visualize the best route from a rapid study of the map, then follow it quickly and accurately. Expert orienteers use many of the techniques I've already described, which in fact originated in the sport. Wherever possible, for example, they look for handrails that lead them in the right direction. Trails and roads are the most obvious handrails; power lines, fences, streams, and edges of fields are less obvious but equally effective. Over a short distance the sun can be a handrail. Perhaps you can follow your shadow or run with the sun full in your face. Or perhaps you can tell from the map that you need to follow a course that crosses the shadows thrown by trees at a 90-degree angle. With a good handrail as a guide, a runner can move out at full speed without wasting time checking map and compass.

As runners near the control, they begin searching for a catching feature crossing their path at 90 degrees to alert them to slow down and begin navigating more carefully. A catching feature can be any of the features described as potential handrails. Once runners locate the intersection of the handrail and the catching feature, they begin searching for the attack point: some relatively easy-to-find landmark close to the control. From there runners follow a precise compass bearing for a distance measured off the map. To keep track of distance, they measure the length of their stride beforehand and then count paces until they locate the control.

Good route-finding involves more than identifying handrails, catching features, and attack points. It also involves decisions about dealing with obstacles like hills, forests, and brush: over, around, or through?

As a rule of thumb, every foot of elevation gain takes as much time as running 12½ feet on the level. If your map's contour interval is 20 feet, then climbing one contour interval takes as much time as running 250 feet on the level. You can use this rule of thumb to estimate whether it's faster to go over a hill or around. Let's say going over the hill involves a climb of three contour intervals (60 feet), or the equivalent of 750 feet of horizontal travel, plus 250 feet of actual horizontal travel as measured on the map. The total is 1,000 feet. If going around the hill takes less than 1,000 feet of running, it's faster to go around. If it takes more than 1,000 feet, go over the top.

Another rule of thumb concerns the extra time required to run through vegetation and brush. Let's say it takes 1 unit of time for you to cover 100 yards on a good trail or road. You can then estimate that it will take you 2 units of time to cover the same distance through tall grass, 3 units of time through forest with light underbrush, and 4 to 6 units of time through heavy underbrush.

If the idea of honing your route-finding skills by finding controls appeals to you but you don't like the competitive aspect, you can attend nearly all meets and amble through the course (or a different one set up especially for people like you) at your own pace, locating the controls and punching your control card with the specially shaped punch found at each control. In orienteering jargon you'll be known as a wayfarer or map-walker. Noncompetitive orienteering is especially popular among families with small kids.

Regular practice is the best way to perfect and maintain your map-and-compass skills. Orienteering meets provide an excellent way to do that in a safe and nonthreatening environment. With your route-finding skills nailed down, you'll be ready to tackle a journey into the deep wilderness, confident you can not only find your way there but also find your way back home again.

APPENDIX

Sources of maps, compasses, altimeters, and GPS receivers

First, some general notes on this appendix. Many companies insist that all customer-service inquiries be handled initially online. You can find e-mail addresses and support-request forms on the companies' websites. Also, please note that websites, phone numbers, and addresses are subject to change. The remedy, of course, is a quick search in your favorite search engine, which is likely to give you the information you seek. Also, while I have provided addresses for these companies, you should always contact customer support by e-mail or phone prior to shipping a damaged or defective product back to the manufacturer. Many manufacturers will require you to obtain a return authorization number in advance and write the number on the outside of the package. The address to which you ship the product may be different from the address below, depending on your location.

Maps

USGS maps are available from the USGS and many private map dealers. You can mail-order maps directly from the USGS using the contact information below.

> USGS Information Services
> Box 25286
> Denver, CO 80225
> (888) ASK-USGS or (303) 202-4700
> Fax: (303) 202-4693
> Website: http://ask.usgs.gov

Order Canadian maps from the Centre for Topographic Information, a division of Natural Resources Canada, using the contact information below.

> Centre for Topographic Information
> Natural Resources Canada
> Customer Support Group
> 2144 King St. W., Suite 010
> Sherbrooke, Quebec J1J 2E8, Canada
> (800) 661-2638 (Canada and United States) or (819) 564-4857
> Fax: (819) 564-5698
> E-mail: topo.maps@NRCan.gc.ca
> Website: http://maps.NRCan.gc.ca

Trails Illustrated, a division of National Geographic, offers maps for popular recreation areas in thirty-five states. These tough, waterproof maps, which are printed on plastic, are based on USGS topos. They're very convenient because they usually cover the entire area you'll traverse in a typical trip with one map. On a trip in Colorado's Indian Peaks Wilderness, for example, you can carry just one Trails Illustrated map instead of four or more 7.5 minute USGS quads. The drawback is that the scale is smaller than on a USGS 7.5 minute quad, so the maps show less detail, which makes precision route-finding more difficult. Trails Illustrated maps are available from even more private map dealers and outdoor shops than USGS 7.5 minute topos.

Trails Illustrated
National Geographic Maps
212 Beaver Brook Canyon Rd.
Evergreen, CO 80439
(800) 962-1643 (United States and Canada) or (303) 670-3457 (elsewhere)
Fax: (800) 626-8676 (United States and Canada) or (303) 670-3644
(elsewhere)
Website: www.natgeomaps.com/trailsillustrated.html

National Geographic also publishes electronic maps through its Topo! division, some of which combine Trails Illustrated maps with the Topo! software. If you can't find them in a local retailer, check out http://shop.nationalgeographic.com/ngs/category/maps/mapping-software.

If you don't like typing in huge URLs, just search for "National Geographic topo maps" or call (800) 437-5521.

Compasses and Altimeter Watches

Most map dealers and outdoor specialty shops carry compasses. If you have trouble finding what you want locally, you can order a compass or get the address of the nearest dealer from the manufacturer or distributor. The big three brands for high-quality compasses for outdoorsmen are Brunton, Silva, and Suunto. Silva and Suunto also make altimeter watches.

For information on Brunton compasses, contact:

Brunton Outdoor Group
2255 Brunton Ct.
Riverton, WY 82501
(307) 857-4700
Website: www.bruntongroup.com

Johnson Outdoors distributes Silva compasses and Silva and Tech4o altimeter watches. For information contact:

Johnson Outdoors Inc.
555 Main St.
Racine, WI 53403
Tech4o Customer Service U.S.A. (US customers for both Silva and Tech4o brands)
(800) 572-8822
Johnson Outdoors Canada (Canadian customers)
(905) 634-0023
Websites: www.silvacompass.com
www.tech4o.com

For information on Suunto compasses and altimeter watches, contact:

Suunto USA
c/o Amer Sports Winter & Outdoor
2030 Lincoln Ave.
Ogden, UT 84401
(800) 543-9124
Website: www.suunto.com

Suunto Canada
85 Davy Rd.
Belleville, Ontario K8N 5B6, Canada
(800) 267-7506 or (613) 966-9220
Website: www.suunto.com

Casio also makes altimeter watches. For information on the many Casio models, contact:

Casio America
570 Mount Pleasant Ave.
Dover, NJ 07801-1620
(800) 836-8580
Website: www.pathfinder.casio.com/watches

GPS Receivers

GPS receivers are so commonplace today that you can even find them at some mass merchandisers. If you can't find the model you want locally, contact the manufacturers.

For DeLorme GPS units contact:

DeLorme
2 DeLorme Dr.
PO Box 298
Yarmouth, ME 04096
(800) 561-5105
Website: www.delorme.com

For Eagle GPS units contact:

Lowrance Electronics
12000 E. Skelly Dr.
Tulsa, OK 74128
(918) 437-6881 or (800) 324-1354
Website: www.lowrance.com

For Garmin GPS units contact:

Garmin International
1200 E. 151st St.
Olathe, KS 66062-3426
(913) 397-8200 or (800) 800-1020 or (866) 429-9296 (Canada)
Website: www.garmin.com

For Magellan GPS units contact:

Magellan
471 El Camino Real
Santa Clara, CA 95050-4300
(800) 707-9971
Website: www.magellangps.com

Orienteering

For more information on the sport of orienteering, contact the United States Orienteering Federation at the following mailing address:

Orienteering USA
PO Box 1444
Forest Park, GA 30298-1444
(404) 363-2110
Website: http://orienteeringusa.org

CHECKLISTS FOR DAY-HIKING, SUMMER BACKPACKING AND WINTER OVERNIGHT TRIPS

This is the checklist I use for summer day-hiking, summer backpacking and winter overnight trips in the Rockies. You'll need to modify it based on personal taste, season and region of the country.

Summer Day Hiking

CLOTHING

- ❏ lightweight socks
- ❏ medium-weight wool socks
- ❏ Gore-Tex socks (in wet terrain)
- ❏ boots
- ❏ convert-a-pants
- ❏ short-sleeve shirt
- ❏ long-sleeve shirt
- ❏ down sweater
- ❏ fleece sweater with hood
- ❏ sun hat with skirt
- ❏ fleece hat
- ❏ light gloves
- ❏ rain pants
- ❏ rain jacket
- ❏ sunglasses

EQUIPMENT

- ❏ headlamp with extra batteries
- ❏ Swiss Army knive
- ❏ water filter
- ❏ first aid kit
- ❏ 2 large, empty stuff sacks for clothing in pack
- ❏ day pack
- ❏ map
- ❏ compass
- ❏ altimeter
- ❏ GPS unit
- ❏ monocular
- ❏ notebook with pen and pencil
- ❏ lip sunscreen
- ❏ bottle of skin sunscreen
- ❏ water bottle(s)
- ❏ toilet paper
- ❏ watch
- ❏ mosquito repellent
- ❏ trekking poles
- ❏ whistle
- ❏ repair kit
- ❏ cell phone
- ❏ plastic bag for trash
- ❏ lunch

ADD FOR SUMMER BACKPACKING

- ❏ sleeping bag
- ❏ sleeping pad

- ❏ tent
- ❏ stove
- ❏ lighters
- ❏ pot with lid
- ❏ pot grips
- ❏ fuel
- ❏ wilderness permit, site map, parking permit (for dash)
- ❏ 75 feet of cord
- ❏ 2 large garbage bags
- ❏ toothbrush, toothpaste and floss
- ❏ bowl
- ❏ spoon
- ❏ mug
- ❏ a few paper towels
- ❏ book
- ❏ repair kit

ADD FOR ONE-DAY WINTER TRIPS

- ❏ thermos or insulating water-bottle sleeve
- ❏ long underwear tops and bottoms
- ❏ fleece bibs
- ❏ down jacket
- ❏ gaiters
- ❏ snowshoes
- ❏ ski poles
- ❏ goggles
- ❏ Neoprene face mask
- ❏ sunglasses
- ❏ heavy mittens

❏ heavy gloves

❏ second pair of light fleece gloves

❏ vapor-barrier socks

❏ double plastic mountaineering boots or pac boots

ADD FOR MULTI-DAY WINTER TRIPS

❏ 1 cup measuring cup (for adding snow to pot)

❏ backcountry shovel

❏ avalanche beacons

❏ vapor-barrier sleeping-bag liner

❏ extra pair of liner socks

❏ second foam pad

❏ six stuff sacks (for use as tent stakes)

ITEMS TO DROP FROM SUMMER LIST FOR WINTER TRIPS

❏ water filter

❏ headnet

❏ mosquito repellent

❏ 75 feet of cord

❏ convert-a-pants

❏ short-sleeve shirt

❏ long sleeve shirt

❏ down sweater

INDEX

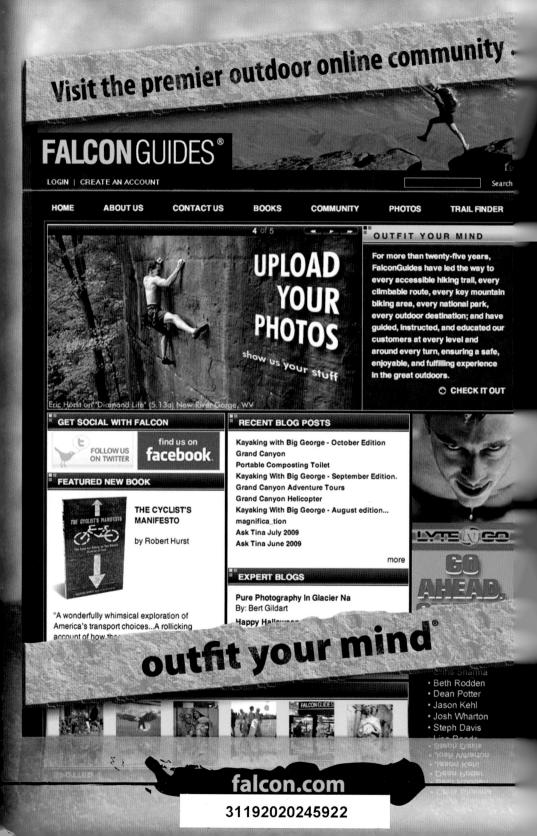

31192020245922